Fodor's
25 Best

VENICE

Contents

KEY TO SYMBOLS

- ✚ Map reference to the accompanying pull-out map
- ✉ Address
- ☎ Telephone number
- 🕐 Opening/closing times
- 🍴 Restaurant or café
- 🚆 Nearest rail station
- 🚌 Nearest bus route
- ⛴ Nearest riverboat or ferry stop

♿ Facilities for visitors with disabilities	🎫 Admission charges: Expensive (over €10), Moderate (€5–€10) and
🛈 Tourist information	Inexpensive (under €10)
❷ Other practical information	
▷ Further information	

Introducing Venice

 Venice, improbably and breathtakingly built on water, has been seducing visitors for centuries. The charms of its cityscape are as potent today as ever, despite the impact of mass tourism, floods and a decreasing population.

The city sits at the heart of a lagoon, its many islands, alleys and canals divided into six districts, or *sestieri*, three to the west of the Canal Grande (San Polo, Dorsoduro and Santa Croce) and three to the east (San Marco, Castello and Cannaregio). Each has its own unmissable sights and each has a maze of timeless alleys and streets—a delight to wander for their own sake.

This labyrinth may initially look intimidating, but the city is easier to navigate than it looks: Distances are short, a few key streets wend through the maze, and the Rialto, Venice's old commercial heart, and the Piazza San Marco, its most famous square, provide central points of reference. On your first morning, though, resist the temptation to dash for the major sights. Start instead with a cappuccino in a sleepy square, or something where the crowds don't turn you away from the city at the first acquaintance.

Then you can move to the bigger draws and finally grapple with what to see among Venice's plethora of wonderful churches, palaces and museums. Don't forget the cafés, walks, tiny shops, and essential boat trips along the Canal Grande or perhaps out to the islands of the lagoon.

However, in seeing the sights, don't fall into the trap of believing Venice is a sort of medieval theme park, a dead city sustained for the benefit of visitors. The population may be falling, but this is an enduring place: a city where people live and work, raise their families and have the same hopes and worries as people everywhere else. Where they differ is in living their everyday lives surrounded by the glories of one of the world's most beautiful cities. The pride they feel in this manifests itself in diverse ways, but it's indubitably this pride that will help to preserve the city and its treasures for generations to come.

FACTS AND FIGURES

- It is estimated that there are 3,000 alleys in Venice. Laid end to end they would stretch for 192km (120 miles).
- Venice has around 400 bridges.
- The city has around 600 tourist shops.
- Fifty percent of the city's workforce is involved in tourism.
- In 1946, the population of central Venice was 110,000; today, it's around 51,000.

SPECIAL TICKETS

The Venezia Unica City Pass (€60.90, ages 6–29 €36.90) is valid for 7 days. It gives access to the Palazzo Ducale, Chorus Group churches, 10 civic museums, an audio-tour to the Fenice and free or reduced entry to many attractions. The San Marco Pass (€33.90) is similar but only includes the museums in and around San Marco. Book online at veneziaunica.it.

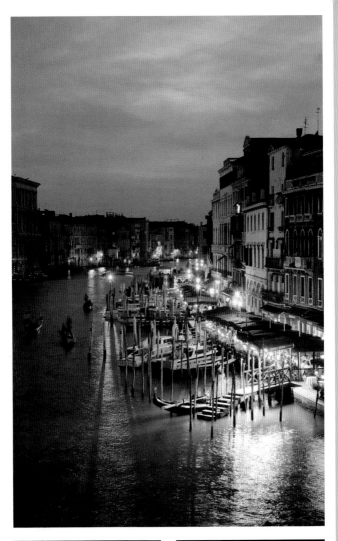

ACQUA ALTA

Visit Venice between November and April and you run the risk of encountering *acqua alta* or "high water," when winter weather, winds and high tides combine to submerge large areas. Raised wooden walkways, *passerelle*, are laid out on key routes to help people get around, and it makes sense to pack knee-high rubber boots.

BEST MOMENTS

These are often away from the main sights. So take a boat along the Canal Grande just for the ride, or see the Rialto markets at the crack of dawn before the crowds arrive. Little beats an aerial view, preferably from the top of San Giorgio Maggiore, and no city offers more to those who wander at random. A trip to the islands off-season can be magical.

Focus on Venice in the 21st Century

With a solid thousand years of tourism under their belts, Venetians are used to reinventing their city's image and, entering into the third decade of the millennium, there's a feeling that once more the balance has shifted.

Visiting Venice

Today's tourists no longer have time to spend a couple of weeks gently exploring; more than 80 percent spend just one day in Venice, pouring into the city from trains, buses and the vast cruise liners whose presence is such a contentious issue for many locals. The others come for perhaps two or three days only, and all of them are more focused on catching the main sights, and enjoying good eating and shopping, than visiting obscure churches.

Saving the City

Given its watery peculiarities, Venice has its own problems it has to deal with if it's to function as a 21st-century city. For far too long, the state of the lagoon and the issues with pollution and flooding were ignored. This changed around 2000, when the vast civic engineering project known as MOSE was launched. Its best-known feature is the huge pontoons, which will rise from the sea floor at the entrances into the lagoon at very high tides to protect the city from flooding. These were due to be operational in 2018, but the project, mired in controversy, is still not complete. However, beaches and dunes have been restored and replanted, the sea walls along the Adriatic strengthened, low-lying quaysides raised, salt marshes reinstated all over the lagoon and 12 eroding islands stabilized.

The industrial complex of Marghera on the west edge of the lagoon has been cleaned up, helping cut the air and water pollution, and it's hoped that by the 2050s Venice will be as secure as possible from decay and floods.

Clockwise from top: A costumed couple walk near Piazza San Marco during Carnavale; boats taking part in the Regata Storica on the Canal Grande in

Getting it Right

Venetians and visitors need a city that really works, not a time capsule, and today things simply function much better. Technology has been enthusiastically embraced and tourists can now plan and book every aspect of their trip online before ever setting foot in Venice via the Venezia Unica app (▷ 163), which will also hold your hand while you're actually in the city.

Transportation has greatly improved to help everyone get around, with the much-loved *vaporetti* (water buses) linking smoothly with buses, trains and a people-mover accessing the city's car parks, while the fourth Grand Canal bridge (Ponte della Costituzione) changed commuters' lives for the better.

Eating and drinking habits have also changed considerably, and Venice now has modern, all-day eateries serving food that's right up to date alongside the more traditional places. The large student population ensures there are plenty of bars, many of which wouldn't look out of place in New York, London or Paris.

Experiences

Today, too, there's a lot more emphasis on the unique experiences that Venice can offer. Of course, there's the gondola ride and the high-end shopping, but there are also guided walks, behind-the-scenes visits to St Mark's Basilica, the Doge's Palace and the Fenice opera house, food and wine city tours or the chance to parade the streets in full 18th-century carnival costume—all captured for you on film. Visitors can learn to row Venetian-style, go jogging, swim in one of the city's pools or, around Christmas, enjoy the open-air ice rink in Campo San Polo.

Increasingly, tourists can create their own Venetian adventure in a city facing the future with confidence.

September; a detail of the Gothic tracery on the facade of Ca' d'Oro; the striking Basilica di San Marco; Riva degli Schiavoni gondola pier; Piazza San Marco at night

Top Tips For...

These great suggestions will help you tailor your ideal visit to Venice, no matter how you choose to spend your time.

Fabulous Views
Take the elevator to the top of the **Campanile** (▷ 36–37) for spectacular, far-reaching views over the rooftops.
The bell tower of **San Giorgio Maggiore** (▷ 42–43) offers sweeping vistas across the entire city.
Climb the tower of the cathedral on **Torcello** (▷ 62–63) for a sweeping panorama of the Venetian lagoon.

Burning the Midnight Oil
Have a drink in one of the cafés and bars on **Campo Santa Margherita** (▷ 67).
Find an atmospheric old wine bar such as **Do Mori** (▷ 136).
Venice has few late-opening nightspots— **Bacaro Jazz** (▷ 135) and **Paradiso Perduto** (▷ 137) are two of the best.

The Lap of Luxury
Splash out on one of Venice's new-wave designer hotels—**Ca' Maria Adele** (▷ 157) typifies this fabulous self-indulgence.
Enjoy an expensive coffee or, better, an aperitif or late drink in **Caffè Florian** (▷ 147), a Venetian institution.
Experience the finest selection of luxury shopping in the sumptuous surroundings of the **Fondaco dei Tedeschi** (▷ 125).

A Breath of Fresh Air
Have a picnic or unwind in the grassy, tree-shaded **Giardini Savorgnan** (▷ 68).
Visit **Torcello** (▷ 62–63) for some bracing sea air.
Verdant **Sant'Erasmo** (▷ 76), Venice's vegetable garden, offers great opportunities for fresh air and country walking.

Clockwise from top: A view down onto Piazza San Marco from the Campanile; Canal Grande seen from the Ponte dell'Accademia; inside a shop selling

Keeping the Children Happy

Take them on plenty of boat rides, especially down the **Canal Grande** (▷ 20–21).
Buy them a mask from **Tragicomica** (▷ 129) or ice cream from **Nico** (▷ 149) or **GROM** (▷ 148).
Visit one of **Murano's glass factories** to see glassblowers in action (▷ 30–31).

Saving for a Rainy Day

Invest in the **San Marco Citypass** (€33.90), which gives access to the Palazzo Ducale, three civic museums and three Chorus Group churches, and offers reductions to a number of other city attractions.

Travel the length of the **Canal Grande**, surely the world's finest journey by public transportation (▷ 20–21, 166–167).
Just €0.60 on a *traghetto* (▷ 167) across the Canal Grande buys you a ride on a gondola.

Specialty Shopping

Many of Venice's high-fashion and other designer stores cluster in and around Calle Larga XXII Marzo, or head for **Tessitura Bevilacqua** (▷ 129) for the beautiful damasks, silks and velvets.

Nothing beats the **Rialto markets** (▷ 41, 128) and the delicatessens in the surrounding streets such as Ruga Vecchia di San Giovanni. Small, specialist stores line the **Mercerie** (▷ 69) and other streets between St. Mark's and the Rialto Bridge. Marbled paper, glass and local foods are popular gift choices.

An Evening on the Town

Take in an opera or concert at **La Fenice** (▷ 75, 138), Venice's opera house.
Contact a tourist office (▷ 167) to find **a concert** in one of Venice's churches or palaces.
Dress up for an evening's lighthearted gambling in Venice's **casino** (▷ 135).

handmade paper; a fruit stall at the Rialto market; Teatro La Fenice; the sumptuous surroundings of Caffè Florian; the green fields on Torcello island

Timeline

800BC Sporadic settlement of the lagoon begun by the Venetii and Euganei tribes.

250BC Rome conquers Venetia and founds important colonies at Padua, Verona, Altinium and Aquileia.

MARCO POLO

Born in Venice in 1254, Marco Polo left with his father in 1269 on a journey that would last two decades. In 1275, he arrived at the court of Kublai Khan, where he served the Mongol emperor until 1295. In 1298, he was captured by the Genoese and it was from prison that he dictated his *Description of the World*.

ANTONIO VIVALDI

Vivaldi was born in Venice in 1678. Although ordained as a priest, he devoted his life to music, teaching violin at La Pietà orphanage, whose girls received music training as part of their state-funded education. La Pietà's orchestra enabled Vivaldi to create a wealth of musical compositions, including his most famous work, *The Four Seasons*.

AD402 Alaric the Goth sacks Altinium and other northeastern colonies. A vision of the Virgin guides refugees to an island in the lagoon.

421 According to legend, Venice is founded on 25 March, the Feast Day of the Virgin Mary.

453 Aquileia is sacked by Attila the Hun, prompting another exodus of refugees to the lagoon.

697 The first Doge (leader) of Venice, Paoluccio Anafesto, is elected.

810 Lagoon dwellers gather on the more easily defended islands of the Rialto.

828 Venetian merchants steal the relics of St. Mark from Alexandria.

1171 Venice's six districts are founded.

1204 Venice sacks Constantinople and acquires much of the former Byzantine Empire.

The Doge sets out in the Bucentaur for the ceremony of Marriage to the Sea (▷ 162)

Piazza San Marco after flooding

1380 Victory over the Genoese at the Battle of Chioggia. Venice wins naval supremacy in the Adriatic and Mediterranean.

1406 Venice defeats Padua and Verona to lay the foundations of a mainland empire.

1453 The Turks take Constantinople.

1498 The discovery of the Cape route to the East weakens Venice's trading monopolies.

1797 Napoleon invades Italy; the last Doge abdicates.

1814 After Napoleon's defeat, the Congress of Vienna cedes Venice and the Veneto to Austria.

1866 Venice joins a united Italy.

1966 Devastating floods draw international attention to the decay of Venice's buildings and artistic treasures; start of major fund-raising for restoration.

2007 Ponte della Costituzione, the fourth bridge over the Canal Grande, opens.

2012 Annual tourist numbers top 17 million; city population falls below 58,000.

2019 MOSE flood barrier partially completed, but is behind schedule and over budget. Oversize cruise ships banned from Giudecca canal. In November, the city suffers the worst floods since 1966, with water levels rising to 187cm (6ft).

COURTESANS AND VENETIAN GREED

At the end of the 16th century, the city contained 11,654 courtesans. This compared with 2,889 patrician women, 1,936 burghers and 2,508 nuns. Taxes from prostitution funded an estimated 12 ships. In the 18th century, according to one contemporary report, "Venetians did not taste their pleasures, but swallowed them whole." Another observer wrote that "the men are women, the women are men, and all are monkeys."

Marco Polo, the great Venetian-born traveler

Crossing Ponte della Costituzione

Top 25

This section contains the must-see Top 25 sights and experiences in Venice. They are listed alphabetically, and numbered so you can locate them on the inside front cover map.

HIGHLIGHTS

● Central door
● Facade mosaics
● Bronze horses
● Rood screen
● Mosaic pavement
● Pala d'Oro
● Interior mosaics

TIPS

● Dress code: no shorts; women must cover shoulders and upper arms.
● From April to October you can pre-book an entry time online.

The perfect architectural fusion of east and west, the great Basilica di San Marco, glittering with mosaics, embodies the might of medieval Venice and the skill of its builders.

St. Mark's resting place The basilica was begun in 832 to house the body of St. Mark, stolen from Alexandria by Venetian merchants four years earlier. For almost 1,000 years it served as the doge's private "chapel" and the city's spiritual heart, accumulating the decorative fruits of a millennium to emerge as the most exotic hybrid of Western and Byzantine architecture in Europe. The original building (destroyed by rioting) was replaced in 978 and again in 1094, the church from the latter date making up most of the one you see today.

Clockwise from far left: The decorated facade above the main door of the basilica; the interior is adorned with mosaics depicting the basilica itself; the basilica lit up at night time; a rooftop detail of the Winged Lion, the symbol of St. Mark

Time to explore Admiring the basilica's treasures is exhausting because there are so many, and because the almost constant crowds can make exploring a challenge. The building remains overwhelmingly striking; spend a few minutes taking in some of the exterior details before plunging inside. These include the *Translation of the Body of St. Mark to the Basilica* (1260–70) above the leftmost door, the west facade's only original mosaic (the rest are later copies) and the superb Romanesque carvings (1240–65) above the central door. Inside, see the famous bronze horses (probably third century AD) in the upper gallery, the view from the Loggia dei Cavalli, the treasury (full of antique silverware), and the Pala d'Oro, an altar screen encrusted with more than 2,600 pearls, rubies, emeralds and other precious stones.

THE BASICS

basilicasanmarco.it

🔛 J6

✉ Piazza San Marco 1, San Marco 30124

☎ 041 270 8311

🕐 Apr–Oct Mon–Sat 9.45–5, Sun 2–5; Nov–Mar 9.45–4.30, Sun 2–4

🍴 Piazza San Marco

🚤 All services to San Marco Vallaresso, San Marco Giardinetti or San Zaccaria

♿ Some steps; uneven floors

🎫 Basilica free. Treasury and Pala d'Oro expensive

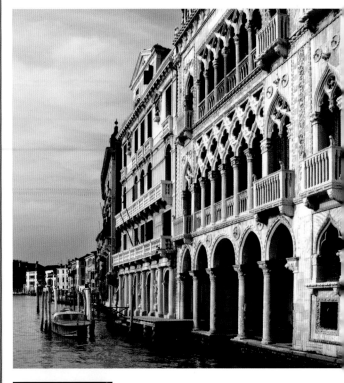

HIGHLIGHTS

- Canal Grande facade
- *Massacre of the Innocents*, artist unknown
- *Crucifixion*, Antonio Vivarini
- *St. Sebastian*, Andrea Mantegna
- *Man and Woman*, busts by Tullio Lombardo
- *The Story of the True Cross*, bronze reliefs by Andrea Briscio
- *Madonna*, Giovanni Bellini
- *Flagellation*, Luca Signorelli

One of the Grand Canal's finest and most flamboyant palazzi, this restored medieval merchant's home and business now houses a finely and carefully curated art collection.

Palace The Ca' d'Oro, or "House of Gold," takes its name from the gilding that once covered its facade; though that has been worn away by wind and rain, the building remains one of the most accomplished pieces of Venetian-Byzantine architecture in the city. The interior, with courtyard, first-floor storage space and grand rooms on the *piano nobile*, is the classic Venetian palazzo layout.

Exhibits Galleria Franchetti, named for the owner who gave his home and collection to the state in 1916, divides into two floors, each

Clockwise from far left: The remarkable exterior of Ca' d'Oro; a detail of Cacciata del Paradiso (Expulsion from the Garden of Eden) *by Giovanni de Sacchis (16th century); people looking out onto the canal from the loggia*

arranged around a central *portego*. On the lower floor, a captivating polyptych of the *Crucifixion* by Antonio Vivarini greets you, along with sculptural fragments belonging to the *Massacre of the Innocents* (14th century). Moving right, you come to the gallery's pictorial masterpiece, Mantegna's sombre *St. Sebastian* (1506). To its left, in the *portego*, are a pair of busts by Tullio Lombardo (15th century), followed by six bronze reliefs, *The Story of the True Cross*, by Andrea Briscio (1470–1532). The rooms off the *portego* contain medallions, a Madonna by Giovanni Bellini and a range of Florentine and Sienese paintings.

More art Upstairs are tapestries, paintings by van Dyck, van Eyck and Tintoretto, and damaged frescoes by Pordenone, Titian and Giorgione.

THE BASICS

cadoro.org

�ᐩ G4

✉ Calle di Ca' d'Oro, Cannaregio 3932, off Strada Nova

☎ 041 520 0345

🕐 Mon 8.15–2, Tue–Sun 8.15–7.15

🚢 Ca' d'Oro N, 1

♿ Poor: stairs

💷 Moderate

HIGHLIGHTS

- Ballroom
- G.B. Tiepolo ceiling frescoes
- Carrera portraits
- Lacquerwork
- Gondola cabin, or *felze*
- Canaletto paintings
- Francesco Guardi paintings
- Pietro Longhi paintings
- G.D. Tiepolo satirical frescoes

If you want a taste of the opulent lifestyle enjoyed by the aristocracy inside a Grand Canal *palazzo*, take a boat to Ca' Rezzonico, once one of the city's most magnificent private houses, now a museum devoted to life, art and style in 18th-century Venice.

How it began The Ca' Rezzonico was begun in 1667 by Baldassare Longhena, a leading architect of his day, but remained half-finished. In 1751, the shell was bought by the Rezzonico family and passed through several hands before opening as a museum in 1936. It begins in fine style in the sumptuous ballroom with *trompe-l'œil* and huge chandeliers. Highlights of the rooms include ceiling frescoes by G.B. Tiepolo, fine lacquerwork, Flemish tapestries and pastel portraits by Rosalba Carrera.

From left: Detail of The Banquet at Casa Nani, Given in Honor of their Guest, Clemente Augusto, Elector Archbishop of Cologne, on 9th September 1755 *by Pietro Longhi, in the gallery's collection; the exterior of the building seen from the Canal Grande*

The collection Much of the palace is devoted to a picture gallery, whose highlight is some paintings by Canaletto, three of only a handful that remain on public display in Venice. Also of interest are Francesco Guardi's views of the city's convents and gambling rooms, together with 39 amateurish but fascinating portraits of Venetian life by Pietro Longhi. Among them is his well-known *Rhinoceros*, painted during the animal's stay in Venice in 1779. Rooms off to the right include a splendid bedchamber, complete with 18th-century closet and sponge-bag. Of special note are a series of satirical frescoes (1793–97) by G.D. Tiepolo, a collection of traditional puppets, three rooms from an old pharmacy, fine clothing enhanced with lace and the excellent views from the palace's upper floors.

THE BASICS

carezzonico.visitmuve.it
+ E6
✉ Fondamenta Rezzonico, Dorsoduro 3136
☎ 041 241 0100
🕐 Apr–Oct Wed–Mon 10.30–6; Nov–Mar Wed–Mon 10.30–4.30. Ticket office closes 1 hour earlier
🍽 Campo San Barnaba
🚤 Ca' Rezzonico 1
♿ Good
💰 Expensive
❓ City Pass (▷ 4)

4 Canal Grande

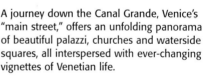

HIGHLIGHTS

- Palazzo Vendramin-Calergi
- San Stae
- Ca' Pesaro (▷ 66–67)
- Ca' d'Oro (▷ 16–17)
- Ponte di Rialto
- Ca' Rezzonico (▷ 18–19)
- Santa Maria della Salute (▷ 52–53)

TIPS

- The *vaporetto* is probably the best way of seeing the canal; gondolas and taxis are far more expensive.
- If time is short take the No. 2, which has fewer stops than the No. 1.

A journey down the Canal Grande, Venice's "main street," offers an unfolding panorama of beautiful palazzi, churches and waterside squares, all interspersed with ever-changing vignettes of Venetian life.

A riot of life and noise Snaking 4km (2.5 miles) through the heart of Venice, the canal divides the city: Three of the city's six districts, or *sestieri*, lie to one side and three to the other. For much of the day and night it is alive with boats and bustle, providing an almost hypnotic spectacle when admired from one of its four bridges (Costituzione, Scalzi, Rialto and Accademia) or from the heavily laden *vaporetti* that ply up and down the canal. The palaces that line its banks, a historical digest of the city's most appealing architecture over 500 years, are

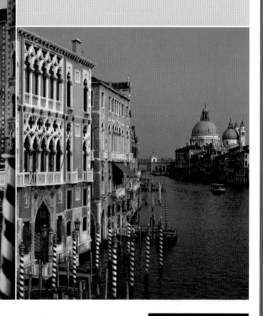

From far left: A busy stretch along the Canal Grande; lights sparkle on the waters on the canal; looking along the canal past striped gondola poles toward Santa Maria della Salute

another attraction. From the Ponte di Rialto, Venice's most famous bridge, you get a view of the canal at its most frantically busy.

Jump on board A trip along this intriguing canal is a pleasure in itself. Board *vaporetto* No. 1 or No. 2 at Piazzale Roma or the Ferrovia (rail station), making sure the boat is heading in the right direction. For the best views, try to secure one of the few outside seats at the front or rear of some boats; Venetians prefer to stand in the middle. The Rialto and Accademia bridges make convenient stops, but for your first trip go all the way to San Marco (and then make the return journey to take in the glory of the palaces on the opposite bank). It is also well worth making the trip at night, when the experience is possibly even more magical.

THE BASICS

- D4–G7
- 1, 2 (year-round)
- Good
- Moderate
- *Vaporetto* 1 halts at every stop; 2 stops at Piazzale Roma, Ferrovia, San Marcuola, Rialto, Sant'Angelo, San Tomà, San Samuele, Accademia, San Marco Vallaresso and San Marco Giardinetti

5 Collezione Peggy Guggenheim

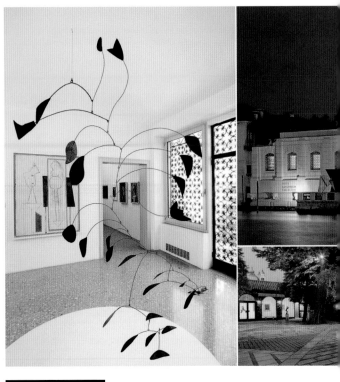

One of Venice's top visitor attractions is a unique and unfinished palazzo on the Canal Grande, which is home to a superb and imaginatively displayed collection of mid-20th-century modern art.

Perfect setting The Guggenheim's small but polished collection was accumulated by Peggy Guggenheim (1898–1979), daughter of an American copper magnate, and installed by her in the 18th-century Palazzo Venier dei Leoni. The collection's appeal owes much to its immaculate presentation as well as to the beauty of its setting, many of the sculptures being arranged in a lovely garden. This has works by Henry Moore, Paolozzi, Giacometti and others, and houses the New Wing and appealing museum store.

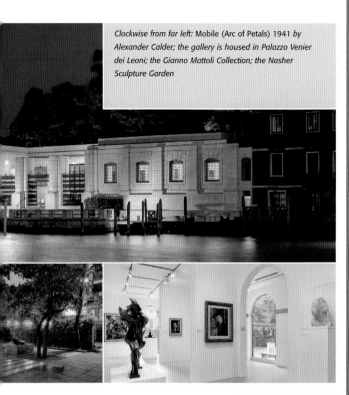

Clockwise from far left: Mobile (Arc of Petals) 1941 by Alexander Calder; the gallery is housed in Palazzo Venier dei Leoni; the Gianno Mattoli Collection; the Nasher Sculpture Garden

Modern art Guggenheim's taste and money allowed her to select high-quality works from virtually every modern art movement of the 20th century. At the same time, she had a penchant for the surreal and avant-garde, having enjoyed a brief relationship with the German surrealist painter Max Ernst. The collection features cubist works by Picasso and Braque, and the surrealism of Dalí, Magritte and Mirò. American modernists here include Jackson Pollock and Mark Rothko, while the English are represented by Francis Bacon. There are sculptures by Calder and Brancusi, as well as works by Italian Futurists Balla and Boccioni from the Gianni Mattioli Collection. The most memorable work is Marino Marini's provocative *Angel of the Citadel*, on the terrace overlooking the Canal Grande.

THE BASICS

guggenheim-venice.it

➕ G7

✉ Palazzo Venier dei Leoni, Calle San Cristoforo, Dorsoduro 701–704

☎ 041 240 5411

🕐 Wed–Mon 10–6

⛴ Salute 1

♿ Good

💶 Expensive

HIGHLIGHTS

● *Madonna and Saints*, Giovanni Bellini
● *Tempest*, Giorgione
● *Supper in the House of Levi*, Veronese
● *The Translation of the Body of St. Mark*. Tintoretto
● *Pietà*, Titian
● Pietro Longhi paintings
● *The Miracles of the True Cross*
● "Life of St. Ursula," Carpaccio

TIPS

● Ongoing restoration will impact the second-floor galleries until 2020/21; check website for details.
● Download the free app, Gallerie dell'Accademia, to make the most of your visit.

Even in a city where art awaits you at every turn, a visit to the Accademia, home to the world's greatest collection of Venetian paintings, is an unmissable experience.

Masterpieces The Accademia began life as Venice's art school in 1750, moving to its present site in 1807 when it garnered much of its permanent collection from churches and religious houses suppressed by Napoleonic decree. The building combines ground-floor state-of-the-art, high-tech exhibition spaces with more traditional galleries above. Some of the gallery's best-known paintings are its Byzantine works, a style that influenced the city's earliest painters. Canvases by Carpaccio, Mantegna, Bellini and others reflect Venice's Renaissance heyday, alongside the Accademia's most

From far left: Miracle of the Slave *and* St. Mark's Body Brought to Venice*, both by Tintoretto; a detail of* Madonna and Child *by Antonio Vivarini;* Madonna and Child with Saints Francis, John the Baptist, Job, Dominic, Sebastian and Louis *by Giovanni Bellini*

famous painting, Giorgione's *Tempest* (c.1500). High Renaissance masterpieces include Veronese's *Supper in the House of Levi* (1573) and Tintoretto's *Miracle of the Slave* and *The Translation of the Body of St. Mark* (c.1560).

Fresco cycles Leave plenty of time for the Accademia's highlights, two *storie*, or fresco cycles. The first, *The Miracles of the True Cross* (1494–1510), was painted by a variety of artists for the Scuola di San Giovanni Evangelista. Each describes a miracle worked by a relic of the "True Cross" owned by the *scuola*, though often the miracle itself takes second place to the fascinating anecdotal detail. The same is true for the second cycle, painted by Carpaccio for the Scuola di Sant'Orsola, with episodes from the "Life of St. Ursula."

THE BASICS

gallerieaccademia.org

⊞ F7

✉ Campo della Carità, Dorsoduro 1050

☎ 041 522 2247; reservations 8000 150 666

🕐 Tue–Sun 8.15–7.15, Mon 8.15–2

🍴 Campo Santo Stefano

🚢 Accademia 1, 2

♿ Poor: some steps

💲 Expensive

HIGHLIGHTS

- Campo di Ghetto Nuovo
- Sinagoga Scuola Levantina
- Sinagoga Scuola Spagnolo
- Holocaust Memorial
- Museo Ebraico

TIPS

- Remember Saturday is the Sabbath and the museum and synagogues are shut to tourists.
- Check out the traditional pastries at Panificio Volpe.

Venice's Ghetto, historically the area where the city's Jews lived, gave its name to every ghetto in history, and still preserves some fascinating synagogues and a museum focusing on the story of Venice's Jews.

Campo di Ghetto Nuovo The Campo, set on its own island, is the heart of the Ghetto—the name comes from the foundries which were once here (*gettare* means "to cast"). From the 16th century, Jews were allowed to live more safely here than anywhere else in Europe. Not that life was easy: Many professions were banned to Jews, they had to wear distinctive badges and were heavily taxed, and the entire Ghetto was gated and guarded between sunset and sunrise. The lovely square is surrounded by tall, narrow buildings, some with up to seven

Clockwise from left: The wooden Ponte di Ghetto Nuovo, leading to a small gateway into the New Ghetto; one of the reliefs of the Holocaust Memorial by Arbit Blatas; the main hall of the Scuola Spagnolo, Venice's largest surviving synagogue

floors to house as many people as possible in this confined area. You'll notice the Holocaust Memorial, with its reliefs commemorating the deportation and extermination of Venice's Jews in World War II. Here too is the Jewish Museum (Museo Ebraico), filled with documents, textiles, silverware and ceremonial objects.

The synagogues The formal establishment of the Ghetto in 1516 led to successive waves of Jewish immigration from all over Europe. Each arriving group built its own synagogue, mainly within existing buildings. Five survive in all, designed by Christian architects, as Jews were forbidden to follow this profession. They used the painted wood, stucco and gilt typical of Christian buildings, making these distinctive places of worship intriguing to visit.

THE BASICS

museoebraico.it

➕ E2

✉ Museo Ebraico and synagogues: Campo di Ghetto Nuovo 2902

☎ Museum 041 715 350

🕐 Museum Jun–Sep Sun–Fri 10–7; Oct–May Sun–Fri 10–5.30. Synagogue tours Sun–Fri hourly 10.30–4.30

🚏 San Marcuola 1, 2; 4.1, 4.2, 5.1, 5.2 Guglie

♿ Poor

🎟 Museum moderate; synagogue tours expensive

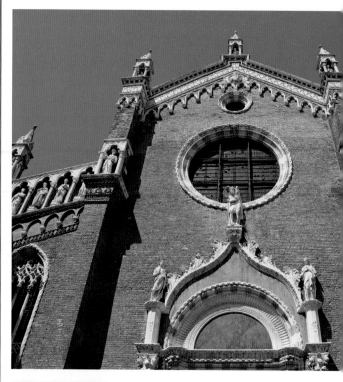

HIGHLIGHTS

- Facade
- Doorway
- *St. Christopher*, Nicolò di Giovanni
- Campanile
- *St. John the Baptist*, Cima da Conegliano
- *Presentation of the Virgin*, Tintoretto
- *The Making of the Golden Calf*, Tintoretto
- *Last Judgment*, Tintoretto
- *St. Agnes Raising Licinius*, Tintoretto (Cappella Contarini)

Madonna dell'Orto ranks high among the many superb Venetian churches. Its lovely setting, off the tourist trail, and graceful red-brick facade are complemented by an airy interior filled with appealing works of art.

Exterior The first church on the present site was founded in 1350 and dedicated to St. Christopher, a statue of whom still dominates the charming brick and stone facade. The building was rededicated to the Virgin in 1377, an act that was inspired by a miracle-working statue of the Madonna found in a nearby vegetable garden *(orto)*. The elegant doorway, by Bartolomeo Bon, is a Renaissance-tinged work. Note the onion dome of the campanile, clear witness to the Byzantine influence on Venetian architecture.

From left: The brick and Istrian stone facade of Madonna dell'Orto church; many of the paintings inside are by Tintoretto, who is buried here along with his children

Interior grandeur Inside, the two aisles contain notable works. The artistic highlights begin in the Contarini Chapel above the first altar on the right, which has Cima da Conegliano's *St. John the Baptist* (1493). At the end of the right nave, above the door, stands Tintoretto's dramatic *Presentation of the Virgin* (1551). In the chapel to the right of the choir lies Tintoretto's tomb (he lived near the church), together with those of his children, Domenico and Marietta. A wall separates the artist from two of his finest paintings, the choir's grand *Last Judgment* and *The Making of the Golden Calf*. Of the three paintings in the apse to the rear, those on the right and left—the *Beheading of St. Paul* and *St. Peter's Vision of the Cross*—are by Tintoretto; the central *Annunciation* is by Palma il Giovane.

THE BASICS

madonnadellorto.org
🚹 G2
✉ Campo Madonna dell'Orto, Cannaregio 3520
☎ 041 795 991
🕐 Mon 10.30–4, Tue–Sat 10.30–4.30
🚤 Orto 4.1, 4.2, 5.1, 5.2
♿ Good
💶 Inexpensive
❓ City Pass (▷ 4)

- Glass factories
- Museo del Vetro
- Santa Maria e Donato

The lagoon island of Murano is a miniature Venice, and has been the heart of Venetian glass production for over 800 years, its peak being between the 15th and 16th centuries.

Seeing Murano It's a 10-minute trip across the lagoon to Murano, a self-contained community with its own Canal Grande, fine churches, palazzi and glass-blowing industry. There are numerous privately run excursions from the city, but for good value and flexibility, make the trip independently via the *vaporetti*. Allow two to three hours for a thorough visit. It's quite feasible, given an early start, to combine a visit to Murano with a trip to the northern islands of Burano and Torcello; study the *vaporetto* timetable with care, as onward connections run half-hourly only.

Clockwise from left: Rio dei Vetrai canal, looking toward San Pietro Martire; the colonnaded facade of the Basilica dei Santi Maria e Donato; a glass-making factory

Highlights The glass factories are well worth a visit but bear in mind the majority are closed on Saturday and Sunday. A glass-making hub since 1291, Murano has three major sights over and above its ubiquitous glass workshops and showrooms. The first is the church of San Pietro Martire, noted for Giovanni Bellini's altarpiece. Also well worth seeing is the Museo del Vetro, Italy's only glass museum, with displays of objects dating from Roman times. Just beyond lies the church of Santi Maria e Donato, distinguished by a striking arched and colonnaded apse. Inside, the 12th-century apse mosaic of the Madonna is outstanding, as are the swirling tinted patterns of the lovely mosaic floor (1141). Don't miss the opportunity to visit a glass workshop or showroom, where you will surely be tempted by items on sale.

THE BASICS

🔲 b2
✉ Isola di Murano
🚤 N, 3, 4.1, 4.2, 12, 13, 18 from Piazzale Roma, Ferrovia and Fondamente Nove

Museo del Vetro
museovetro.visitmuve.it
🔲 b2
✉ Fondamenta Giustinian 8
☎ 041 243 4914
🕐 Apr–Oct daily 10.30–6; Nov–Mar daily 10–4.30. Ticket office closes 30 mins earlier
🏛 Museo
💲 Expensive

Santi Maria e Donato
🔲 c2
✉ Campo San Donato
🕐 Mon–Sat 9–12, 3.30–7, Sun 3.30–7
🏛 Museo
💲 Free

HIGHLIGHTS

● Aerial view of Venice (1500), Jacopo de' Barbari
● *Daedalus and Icarus*, Canova
● *Two Women*, Carpaccio
● *The Man in the Red Hat*, Lorenzo Lotto (attributed)
● *Pietà*, Antonello da Messina
● *Madonna and Child*, Giovanni Bellini

The splendid rooms of the Museo Correr, overlooking two sides of Piazza San Marco, are home to a fine museum focusing on the history of Venice, and a superb collection of art and classical sculpture.

Fascinating overview Much of the collection here was accumulated by Abbot Teodoro Correr, a Venetian worthy, and bequeathed to the city in 1830. It was immediately housed in the buildings on the south side of Piazza San Marco, previously used as imperial apartments during the French occupation (1797–1814). Today these sumptuous rooms form part of a visit, and lead to the key historic galleries, devoted to exhibits on Venetian history. Don't miss the Wunderkammer, which displays every type of exquisite *objets d'art* collected by

From far left: A fresco of three dancing girls decorates the interior; the opulent ballroom, decorated in Empire style; Doge Giovanni Mocenigo by Gentile Bellini (c.1478)

18th-century aristocrats. Also take time to visit the classical collections in the archeological section, or the superb Biblioteca Marciana, a library designed by Sansovino in 1591.

More art One of the main sections of the museum consists of a large hall devoted to several fine sculptures by Antonio Canova. Occupying the top floor is the city's second-finest art gallery after the Accademia. Its most popular picture is Carpaccio's *Two Women* (1507), a masterful study of ennui once known as *The Courtesans* for the plunging necklines. Other well-known paintings include *The Man in the Red Hat* (by either Carpaccio or Lorenzo Lotto), a *Pietà* by Antonello da Messina and works by Cosmè Tura, Alvise Vivarini, and Jacopo, Giovanni and Gentile Bellini.

THE BASICS

correr.visitmuve.it

➕ H6

✉ Procuratie Nuove, Ala Napoleonica, Piazza San Marco 52, San Marco 30124

☎ 041 240 5211

🕐 Apr–Oct daily 10–7; Nov–Mar 10.30–5. Ticket office closes 1 hour earlier

🍴 Piazza San Marco

🚤 San Marco Vallaresso, San Marco Giardinetti N, 1, 2

♿ Poor

💲 Expensive

❓ City Pass (▷ 4)

HIGHLIGHTS

- Bridge of Sighs
- Tetrarchs
- Porta della Carta
- Scala dei Giganti
- Arco Foscari
- Sala dell'Anticollegio
- Sala del Collegio
- Sala del Maggior Consiglio
- Armory and prisons

TIP

- Winter visitors should dress warmly as there is no heating and it can be very cold.

Italy has a host of beautiful Gothic buildings, but the Palazzo Ducale is by far the most captivating: the seat of the doge and home to Venice's various offices of state for almost a thousand years.

Evolution The first ducal palace, completed in 814, was a severe fortress built on one of the few clay redoubts in the lagoon. This burned down in 976, as did its successor in 1106. By 1419 the palace was in its third—and final—incarnation. Three years later, the great hall, or Sala del Maggior Consiglio, was completed—one of many additions made to the interior. By 1550 most work had been completed, only to be undone by fires in 1574 and 1577, conflagrations that not only destroyed masterpieces by some of Venice's greatest painters,

Clockwise from far left: Ponte dei Sospiri (Bridge of Sighs); a view along the outside of the building; the Scala d'Oro (gold staircase) in the palazzo; the astrological clock in the Sala Senato

but also threatened the entire building with collapse. Restoration work continued on and off until the 1880s.

Details Outside is the famous Ponte dei Sospiri (Bridge of Sighs), tucked down a canal at the palace's eastern end, and the fine corner sculptures. Don't miss the excellent carving of the pillars and capitals, and the palace's superb main doorway, the Porta della Carta (1438–43), with the famous little knights, or tetrarchs, to its left. An ornate staircase leads up several flights to the beginning of a marked route leading from one lavishly decorated room to the next. Look for works by Tintoretto, Veronese and other Venetian masters. Tintoretto's gargantuan *Paradiso* (1588–92), the world's largest oil painting, is in the Sala del Maggior Consiglio.

THE BASICS

palazzoducale.visitmuve.it

⊞ J6

✉ Piazzetta San Marco, San Marco 30124

☎ Palace and booking for guided tours 041 271 5911

🕐 Apr–Oct Sun–Thu 8.30am–9pm, Fri–Sat 8.30am–11pm; Nov–Mar daily 8.30–7. Ticket office closes 1 hour earlier

🍴 Palace café

🚢 All services to San Zaccaria, San Marco Vallaresso or San Marco Giardinetti

♿ Poor: steps to upstairs

💲 Expensive

❓ City Pass (▷ 4)

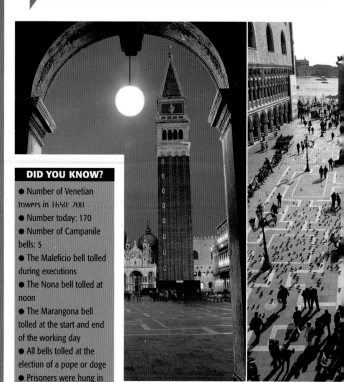

TOP 25

DID YOU KNOW?

- Number of Venetian towers in 1650: 200
- Number today: 170
- Number of Campanile bells: 5
- The Maleficio bell tolled during executions
- The Nona bell tolled at noon
- The Marangona bell tolled at the start and end of the working day
- All bells tolled at the election of a pope or doge
- Prisoners were hung in cages from the Campanile
- Elevator added in 1962

HIGHLIGHTS

Piazza
- Basilica di San Marco (▷ 14–15)
- Palazzo Ducale (▷ 34–35)
- Museo Correr (▷ 32–33)
- Procuratie
- Libreria Sansoviniana
- Torre dell'Orologio (▷ 75)
- Zecca
- Caffè Florian (▷ 147)

Nothing can prepare you for the wonder of emerging from the tightly packed, narrow streets into the vast open space of Piazza San Marco, with its breathtaking backdrop of the Basilica and the soaring campanile.

Hordes Europe's "drawing room" was how Napoleon described Venice's main square, though glancing at today's crowds he would probably be less complimentary. Arrive early or late, however—or off-season—and the piazza can still work its considerable charms. Over and above the obvious sights and (expensive) cafés, make a point of taking in the Zecca (mint), the Procuratie (administrative offices), the underrated Museo Correr, and the Libreria Sansoviniana, considered one of the greatest buildings of its day. Also look for the Torre

From far left: The view through an arch to Basilica di San Marco and the Campanile; looking down on the Piazzetta; from the Campanile there is a good view toward the island of Murano

dell'Orologio and the two granite columns, topped by San Teodoro and the lion of St. Mark, on the waterfront beside the Palazzo Ducale.

Campanile Take the elevator up San Marco's detached bell tower for the views, which can stretch as far as the Alps. The original campanile, which at 98.5m (323ft) was the city's tallest building, dated from the 11th century. Erosion and shallow foundations (20m/66ft deep) proved the tower's undoing and, on July 14, 1902, it collapsed, though there were no casualties. It was rebuilt, as the Venetians insisted, *dov'era e com'era*—"where it was and how it was"—and opened on April 25, 1912, exactly 1,000 years after its predecessor. This time, though, it was 650 tons lighter and supported by an extra 1,000 foundation piles.

THE BASICS

basilicasanmarco.it

➕ H6–J6

🍴 Caffè Florian (▷ 147)

🚤 San Marco Vallaresso, San Marco Giardinetti N, 1, 2, 4, or all services to San Zaccaria

♿ Good

🏛 Museo Archeologico moderate

Campanile

basilicasanmarco.it

☎ 0141 270 8311

🕐 Apr 1–15 daily 9–5.30; Apr 16–Sep daily 8.30am–9pm; Oct–Jan 7, Jan 24–Mar 31 daily 9.30–5. Closed for maintenance Jan 7–24. Book online Apr–Oct to avoid lines

♿ Poor: narrow access to elevator

🏛 Expensive

HIGHLIGHTS

● The main exhibition hall and stairway
● The view over the Basin of St. Mark from the Punta della Dogana
● The Torrino

TIPS

● Allow time to enjoy the building as well as the art.
● There's an excellent bookshop and pleasant café/bar within the complex.

Venice's most exciting contemporary art space, wonderfully positioned where the Canal Grande opens into St. Mark's Basin, showcases cutting-edge, 21st-century art in a converted 17th-century building.

The history The buildings of the Dogana di Mare, Venice's historic customs house, stand at the tip of Dorsoduro, the Punta della Dogana, where the Giudecca Canal merges with the Canal Grande. These warehouses, culminating in a tower and portico, were designed by Giuseppe Benoni and built between 1677 and 1682. Neglected for years, in 2007 the buildings were leased by the city to François Pinault, owner of the Palazzo Grassi (▷ 70). In June 2009, after a €20 million restoration, the 3,440sq m (37,000sq ft) space opened as

Clockwise from left: Punta della Dogana, right at the tip of Dorsoduro; the weathervane on top of the tower, Fortune standing on a globe; the old brick walls of the customs house; modern exhibition space

a permanent contemporary art museum, its interior transformed by Japanese minimalist architect Tadao Ando. Inspired by traditional vernacular architecture, the interior fuses the old brick and stone with steel, glass and concrete.

The galleries Pinault's personal vision and taste dictate much of what's on show—an evolving display that he views as an ongoing project, featuring works from his collection, commissioned pieces from up-and-coming artists, and important temporary exhibitions. Among the former, works by Richard Prince, Rachel Whiteread, Jeff Koons and Cindy Sherman have been on show. The violence inherent in some contemporary work is disturbing, but the Punta della Dogana has brought a new vibrancy to the Venetian art scene.

THE BASICS

palazzograssi.it

➕ H7

✉ Campo di Salute, Dorsoduro 2

☎ 041 200 1057

🕐 Daily 10–7

🍴 Museum café serving snacks and light meals

🚢 Salute

♿ Good

💰 Expensive

● The Ponte di Rialto
● The Pescheria (fish market)
● The produce stalls

TIP

● Remember the fish market is closed on Monday and there are no markets on Sunday.

The Ponte di Rialto, one of Venice's most iconic sights, spans the Canal Grande to link the *sestiere* of San Marco with the Rialto, once the city's commercial hub and still home to the main food markets.

The Ponte di Rialto The *rivo alto*, the "high bank," was one of the firmest areas of the lagoon, so it's no surprise that the first settlements of Venice grew up here, the district becoming the commercial heart of the city. The two banks were linked by a pontoon bridge and the first permanent wooden structure went up in the 13th century. Merchants traded European goods with exotic imports from the East, while international banks and trading companies influenced prices across the known world. This monopoly ceased in 1498, when

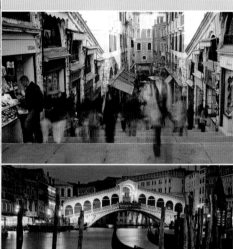

Clockwise from far left: The beautiful Ponte di Rialto; a stall in the fish market on the Rialto; looking across the bridge toward Campo San Bartolomeo; the bridge lit at night

Vasco da Gama rounded the Cape and opened up sea routes to India and the Far East. The present bridge (1588–91) was designed by Antonio da Ponte, who won the commission in a competition, beating architects Palladio and Sansovino. The shops are later additions.

The markets The Rialto is still a trading center, though today the accent is on food, with the open areas crammed with fish, fruit and vegetable stalls. The surrounding streets, whose evocative names recall the commodities traded here, house some of the city's best grocers, butchers, bakers, dairy shops and delicatessens. There's no better way to appreciate Venice as a living city than to join the morning shoppers and enjoy the sights, scents and sounds of one of Europe's most colorful markets.

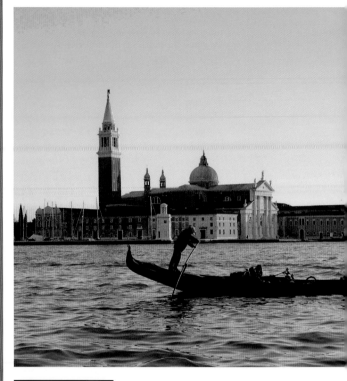

HIGHLIGHTS

- Facade (1559–80)
- Lighthouses (1828)
- Campanile (1791)
- *Adoration of the Shepherds*, Jacopo Bassano
- *The Fall of Manna*, Tintoretto
- *The Last Supper*, Tintoretto
- Choir
- View from the campanile

If asked, many Venetians would probably nominate the view from the bell tower of San Giorgio Maggiore, a magnificent Palladian church on its own island near the Giudecca, as the city's finest.

Classical The church's dazzling marble facade provides one of the great panoramic set pieces of the Venetian skyline. Originally founded in 790, the first church on the site was destroyed by an earthquake in 1223, together with an adjoining Benedictine monastery built in 982 and donated to the order by the doge.

While the monastery was rebuilt in 1443, the church had to wait over a hundred years until 1559 and the arrival of the great Vicenzan architect, Andrea Palladio. His design for the new church adopted many of the architectural

From left: A gondola passes in front of the church of San Giorgio Maggiore, with its bell tower to the left of the picture; the view from the bell tower across the lagoon

idioms of the ancient world (notably the majestic four-column portico) to produce one of Italy's most beautiful neoclassical buildings.

Interior The ancient world also influenced the sparse interior, where light is introduced by high windows, a device borrowed from the bathhouses of third-century Rome. The major works of art are Jacopo Bassano's *Adoration of the Shepherds* (1582), above the second altar on the right, and a pair of outstanding paintings by Tintoretto—*The Fall of Manna* (1594) and *The Last Supper* (1594)—on the walls of the chancel. Behind the high altar is the choir (1594–98), with its impressive wooden stalls, and down a corridor off the north aisle is the elevator up the campanile. The trip to San Giorgio is worth it for the views alone.

THE BASICS
⊞ K8
✉ Campo San Giorgio, Isola di San Giorgio Maggiore
☎ 041 522 7827
⏰ Apr–Oct daily 9–7; Nov–Mar daily 8.30–6
🍴 Giudecca
🚆 San Giorgio N, 2
♿ Poor
🔔 Campanile moderate

PAVLO CALIARIO VERONEN PICTORI
NAT°A. AEMVLO ARTIS MIRACVLO
SV EREST VE FAT'S FAMA VICTVRO

HIGHLIGHTS

- Sacristy
- Ceiling
- Choir and nuns' choir
- Organ
- *St. Nicholas* (1563), Titian (first chapel on right)
- *Madonna and Child* (16th century), Tommaso Lombardo (second chapel on right)
- *Tomb of Archbishop Podocattaro of Cyprus* (d.1555), Sansovino (fourth chapel on right)

While paintings by some of Venice's artists—notably Titian and Tintoretto—are often showcased in grandiose settings, the city's finest collection of works by Veronese is in the humble little church of San Sebastiano.

Veronese Born in Verona, Paolo Caliari Veronese (1528–88) moved to Venice while he was in his twenties, settling close to San Sebastiano, which became his parish church. In 1555, he was commissioned to decorate the sacristy, where he left paintings of the *Evangelists* and the *Coronation of the Virgin*. Impressed by his work, the church authorities gave him free rein to decorate the ceiling. The three main panels depict episodes from the story of Esther, chosen for its symbolic parallels with the stories of Eve and the Virgin Mary.

Clockwise from far left: A bust of Veronese in the church; the facade of San Sebastiano; detail of the Coronation of the Virgin by Veronese, which adorns the sacristy; Cherubi, also by Veronese, is part of the decoration on the ceiling

Monopoly Veronese also painted the high altarpiece—the *Madonna and Child with Saints Sebastian, Peter, Francis and Catherine* (1570)—and the two vast paintings on the north and south walls. The latter portray *Saints Mark and Marcellinus Led to Martyrdom and Comforted by St. Sebastian* and *The Second Martyrdom of St. Sebastian* (Sebastian survived his first assault by arrows and was martyred by being pummelled to death). Veronese also painted *The Trial and Martyrdom of St. Sebastian* in the nuns' choir, above the church's west end. He even designed and painted the organ.

His decorative monopoly of San Sebastiano makes it only fitting that he was buried here. His tomb, and that of his brother, lie in front of the chapel.

THE BASICS

chorusvenezia.org

➕ D7

✉ Campo San Sebastiano, Dorsoduro 1686

☎ 041 275 0462

🕐 Mon–Sat 10.30–4.30

🍴 Campo Santa Margherita and Campo San Barnaba

🚤 San Basilio N, 2, 6, 8

♿ Good

💵 Inexpensive

❓ Chorus Group Pass and City Pass (▷ 4)

HIGHLIGHTS

- Facades
- Martial bas-reliefs
- Plaque recording 1916 incendiary bomb
- Campanile's stone mask
- Interior
- *Madonna della Misericordia*, Bartolomeo Vivarini
- *Santa Barbara*, Palma il Vecchio

A pleasing mix of architectural styles, the ancient foundation of Santa Maria Formosa stands on one of Venice's most archetypal campi, a rambling open space lined with palaces and cafés and vibrant with local life.

The structure This church takes its name from *una Madonna formosa*, "a buxom Madonna," which appeared to St. Magnus in the seventh century, instructing him to follow a small white cloud and build a church wherever it settled. The present building, completed in 1492, was grafted onto an 11th-century Byzantine church, from which it borrowed its Greek-cross plan, a common feature of Byzantine (and later) churches dedicated to the Virgin. The facade (1542) was paid for by the Cappello family, hence its statue of Vincenzo Cappello, a

TOP 25

Venetian admiral. Note the carved face on the bell tower to the left, one of Venice's most famous grotesques.

Interior The church's interior is a unique blend of Renaissance decoration and ersatz Byzantine cupolas, barrel vaults and narrow-columned screens. Of particular interest are two paintings. Tthe first is Bartolomeo Vivarini's *Madonna della Misericordia* (1473), a triptych in the first chapel on the right (south) side. It was financed by the church's congregation, which is depicted in the picture sheltering beneath the Virgin's protective cloak. The second and more famous picture, Palma il Vecchio's *Santa Barbara* (1522–24), depicts the patron saint of artillerymen, and portrays the artist's daughter as its model.

THE BASICS

chorusvenezia.org

⊞ J5

✉ Campo Santa Maria Formosa, Castello 5263

☎ 041 275 0462

🕐 Mon–Sat 10.30–4.30

🍴 Campo Santa Maria Formosa

🚢 San Zaccaria 1, 2, 4.1, 4.2, 5.1, 5.2; Rialto 1, 2

♿ Good

🎟 Inexpensive

❓ Chorus Group Pass and City Pass (▷ 4)

HIGHLIGHTS

- *Madonna and Child*, Giovanni Bellini
- *Assumption*, Titian
- *Madonna di Ca' Pesaro*, Titian
- *Madonna and Child* (1339), Paolo Veneziano (sacristy)
- *St. John the Baptist*, Donatello
- *Mausoleo Tiziano* (Tomb of Titian)
- Wooden choir (124 stalls)
- *Monumento al Doge Giovanni Pesaro*
- *Monumento al Canova*

If you were allowed to walk away with just one work of art from Venice it could well be Bellini's sublime altarpiece in this church, the largest and most important in the city.

Magnificent edifice The Frari narrowly outranks Santi Giovanni e Paolo in size and importance. Founded around 1250, it became the mother church of the city's Franciscans, for whom it is named—*frari* is a Venetian corruption of *frati*, meaning "friars."

The greats interred Many of the city's great and good are buried in the church, among them the painter Titian (d.1576), whose 19th-century tomb occupies the second altar on the right (south) wall. Opposite, on the left wall, stands the *Monumento al Canova*

Clockwise from far left: Bellini's astonishingly detailed triptych (1488), depicting the Madonna and Child with saints and angels; carved wooden inlaid stalls in the Gothic-Renaissance choir; St. John the Baptist by Jacopo Sansovino; the tomb of Doge Francesco Dandelo

(1827), an unmistakable marble pyramid that contains the sculptor's heart. The composer Claudio Monteverdi (d.1643) is buried in the third chapel to the left of the high altar.

Art Titian's compelling and stylistically innovative *Assumption* (1516–18) above the high altar immediately draws your eye; don't miss the same artist's influential *Madonna di Ca' Pesaro* (1526), near the north door. The church's most beautiful painting, however, is Giovanni Bellini's glorious triptych of the *Madonna and Child between Sts. Nicholas, Peter, Mark and Benedict* (1488), in the sacristy. In the first chapel on the right of the high altar you will find Donatello's statue of *St. John the Baptist* (1438), the only work in Venice by the famous Florentine sculptor.

THE BASICS

chorusvenezia.org

➕ E5

✉ Campo dei Frari 3072, San Polo 3072

☎ 041 275 0462

🕐 Mon–Sat 9–6, Sun 1–6. Last admittance 5.30

🍴 Campo dei Frari

🚤 San Tomà N, 1, 2

♿ Good: one or two steps

💷 Inexpensive

❓ Chorus Group Pass (▷ 4)

HIGHLIGHTS

- Tinted marbles
- Decorative inlays
- False pillars
- Bas-reliefs
- Nuns' choir
- Balustrade
- Pillar carving
- Raised choir
- *Madonna and Child*, Nicolò de Pietro
- Ceiling

You'll soon get used to being brought up short in Venice by surprises and views around almost every corner, but none of them quite compares with your first glimpse of the beautiful marbles of Santa Maria dei Miracoli.

Miracles The church was built to house an image of the Virgin, painted in 1409 and originally intended to be placed on the outside of a house (a common practice in Venice). Miracles *(miracoli)* began to be associated with the image in 1480, leading to a flood of votive donations that enabled the authorities to commission a church for the icon from Pietro Lombardo. One of the leading architects of his day, Lombardo created a building that relied for its effect almost entirely on shades,

From left: The unusual interior makes much use of marble and is decorated with statues by the architect Pietro Lombardo and his sons; Lombardo also used marble to great effect on the exterior of the church

hues and tints, facing his church in a variety of honey-toned marbles, porphyry panels and serpentine inlays.

Interior grandeur Lombardo's innovative use of marble continues on the inside, which is filled with an array of sculptures that were executed in tandem with his sons, Tullio and Antonio. The best include the carving on the two pillars that support the nuns' choir (near the entrance); on the half-figures of the balustrade fronting the raised choir; and among the exotica at the base of the choir's pillars. The striking ceiling portrays *50 Saints and Prophets* (1528), by Pier Pennacchi and his assistants. Nicolò di Pietro's *Madonna and Child*, the miraculous image for which the church was built, adorns the high altar.

THE BASICS

chorusvenezia.org

✚ J4

✉ Campo dei Miracoli, Cannaregio 6075

☎ 041 275 0462

🕐 Mon–Sat 10.30–4.30

🍴 Campo Santa Maria Nova

🚤 Rialto N, 1, 2

♿ Good

💶 Inexpensive

❓ Chorus Group Pass and City Pass (▷ 4)

20 Santa Maria della Salute

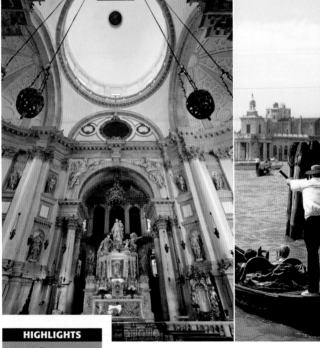

● Marble floor
● *Descent of the Holy Spirit*, Titian
● *The Virgin Casting out the Plague*, Juste le Court
● *Feast at Cana* (1561), Tintoretto (sacristy)
● *Cain and Abel* (1542–44), Titian (sacristy)
● *David and Goliath* (1542–44), Titian (sacristy)
● *Sacrifice of Abraham* (1542–44), Titian (sacristy)
● *St. Mark Enthroned between Sts. Cosmas, Damian, Roch and Sebastian* (1510), Titian (sacristy)

In a city where almost every street and canal offers a memorable vista, this church, proudly situated at the entrance to the Canal Grande, forms part of the famous panorama most people commonly associate with Venice.

Plague In 1630, Venice found itself ravaged by an outbreak of the plague so devastating that the Senate promised to build a church in celebration of the Virgin if she could save the city. Within weeks the pestilence had abated and, on April 1 the following year, the first stone of the Salute, meaning "health" and "salvation" in Italian, was laid. Its architect was Baldassare Longhena.

His design proved to be a baroque model for years to come, combining the Palladian

Clockwise from far left: Santa Maria della Salute has been listed as a World Heritage Site by UNESCO; the church seen from the Grand Canal; the interior of the dome; a view of a circular detail and statue on the exterior

influence of his master, Vincenzo Scamozzi (Andrea Palladio's closest follower), with a range of personal innovations.

Baroque interior The Salute's main impact is as a distant prospect, its dazzling exterior detail and great dome (fashioned on St. Peter's in Rome) forming irreplaceable elements of the Venetian skyline. The interior is more restrained, and its fine marble floor first catches the eye. Moving left from the side entrance, the third of the three altars has an early work by Titian, the *Descent of the Holy Spirit* (1550). The high altar supports *The Virgin Casting out the Plague* (1670), a sculpture designed by Longhena and carved by Juste le Court. The supplicant figure represents Venice, while the elderly harridan moving off right symbolizes the plague.

THE BASICS

basilicasalutevenezia.it

✚ G7/H7

✉ Campo della Salute, Dorsoduro

🕐 Daily 9–12, 3–5.30

🚢 Salute 1

♿ Poor: several steps

🎫 Church free. Sacristy inexpensive

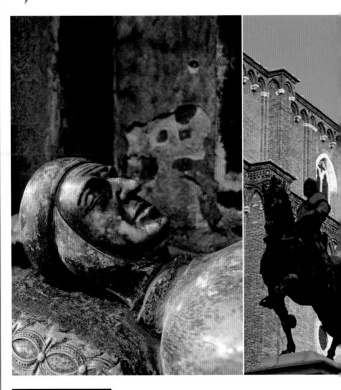

HIGHLIGHTS

- Main portal
- *Monument to Doge Pietro Mocenigo*, Pietro Lombardo
- *St. Vincent Ferrer*, Giovanni Bellini
- *St. Antonius Pierozzi Giving Alms to the Poor*, Lorenzo Lotto
- *Monument to Doge Michele Morosini*
- Veronese ceiling paintings, Cappella del Rosario
- Capella della Madonna della Pace

Nowhere in Venice is there a greater collection of superb sculpture under one roof than in this majestic Gothic church. The walls here are lined with the funerary monuments of more than 20 of the city's important doges.

Monuments Santi Giovanni e Paolo, known locally as San Zanipolo, is rivaled only by Santa Maria Gloriosa dei Frari (▷ 48–49). Its appeal rests on a handful of superb paintings, its tremendous tombs, and on surroundings that include the magnificent facade of the adjacent Scuola Grande di San Marco and Verrocchio's great equestrian statue of Bartolomeo Colleoni. The church was begun in 1246 by Doge Giacomo Tiepolo, who is buried in the most ornate of the four wall tombs built into the

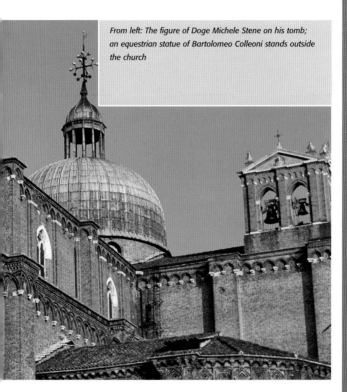

From left: The figure of Doge Michele Stene on his tomb; an equestrian statue of Bartolomeo Colleoni stands outside the church

facade. Inside, further tombs lie around the walls, many by some of Venice's finest medieval sculptors. The best include the monuments to Doge Pietro Mocenigo (d.1476) by Pietro, Tullio and Antonio Lombardo (left of the main door), and to Doge Michele Morosini (d.1382), on the wall to the right of the high altar.

Paintings The most outstanding of the church's paintings are Giovanni Bellini's beautiful and recently restored polyptych of St. Vincent Ferrer (1464, second altar on the right) and the works in the south transept, which include *The Coronation of the Virgin*, attributed to Cima da Conegliano, and Lorenzo Lotto's wonderful *St. Antonius Pierozzi Giving Alms to the Poor* (1542).

THE BASICS

basilicasantigiovannie
paolo.it

J4

Campo Santi Giovanni
e Paolo, Castello 6363

041 523 5913

Mon–Sat 9–6, Sun
12–6.30

Campo Santi Giovanni
e Paolo

Fondamente Nove or
Ospedale 4.1, 4.2, 5.1, 5.2

Good: one step

Inexpensive

HIGHLIGHTS

● Facade
● Stucco staircase
● Ceiling paintings
● Albergo and Archivio
● *Judith and Holofernes*, Piazzetta
● *St. Nicholas of Bari*, Lorenzo Lotto
● *Nativity*, Cima da Conegliano

Giovanni Battista Tiepolo's Rococo-style paintings in the intimate Scuola dei Carmini, all pastel shades and dazzling foreshortening, are a marked contrast to the drama of Titian or Tintoretto.

Carmelites The Carmelite Order's Venetian chapter was originally installed in Santa Maria del Carmelo (or dei Carmini), the Carmelite church just to the left of the *scuola*. In 1667, the order commissioned Baldassare Longhena to design a new home in the present building (Longhena also designed Santa Maria della Salute and a number of palaces on the Canal Grande).

Exuberant ceilings The highlights are Giovanni Battista Tiepolo's nine ceiling paintings

From left: Flight of Angels by Sebastiano Ricci, an older contemporary of Tiepolo; the Sala dell'Archivio with its beautiful polychrome marble floor

(1739–44) in the Salone. The paintings' central panel depicts the vision of St. Simon Stock, elected the Carmelites' prior-general in 1247, in which the Virgin appears to the saint with a "scapular." This garment of two linked pieces of cloth became central to Carmelite belief as wearers were promised relief from the pains of purgatory on the "first Sunday after death." Two adjacent rooms, the Albergo and Archivio, have heavy wooden ceilings and several paintings, the best of which is Piazzetta's *Judith and Holofernes* (1743).

Chiesa dei Carmini Be sure to visit the church to see Lorenzo Lotto's *St. Nicholas of Bari* (1529), by the side door (second chapel), and Cima da Conegliano's fine *Nativity* (1509) above the second altar on the (south) wall.

THE BASICS

scuolagrandecarmini.it

➕ D6

✉ Campo dei Carmini, Campo Santa Margherita, Dorsoduro 2617

☎ 041 528 9420

🕐 Daily 11–5

🍴 Campo Santa Margherita

🚤 Ca' Rezzonico 1

♿ Poor: stairs to main rooms

💷 Moderate

Chiesa dei Carmini

🕐 Mon–Sat 2.30–5.30

💷 Free

- *Crucifixion*
- *Moses Strikes Water from the Rock*
- *The Fall of Manna*
- *The Temptation of Christ*
- *The Adoration of the Shepherds*
- Wooden sculptures
- *The Flight into Egypt*
- *Annunciation*

TIPS

- Allow 1 to 2 hours for a thorough visit.
- Start your visit upstairs in the Albergo.

In a city of superlative and striking works of art, there can be few that make such a marked and powerful first impression as the colossal cycle of 54 paintings by Tintoretto that line the walls here.

From rags to riches This *scuola*, formerly a charitable institution for the sick, was founded in 1478 in praise of St. Roch, whose efficacy against disease made him very popular in pestilence-ridden Venice. In 1564, as one of wealthiest fraternities, the *scuola* instigated a competition to decorate its hall. The winner, Tintoretto, spent some 23 years creating one of Europe's greatest painting cycles.

The wonders inside To see Tintoretto's 54 paintings in the order they were painted,

Clockwise from far left: Detail of the Crucifixion *(1565), one of a series of 54 paintings by Tintoretto; the* Annunciation, *also by Tintoretto; the exterior of the building; the heavily decorated Upper Great Hall in the* scuola

ignore the canvases on the ground level and in the main hall (Sala Grande) upstairs. Instead, go to the Sala dell'Albergo (off the main hall), dominated by a huge *Crucifixion* (1565), often described as one of Italy's greatest paintings. The room's central ceiling panel is *St. Roch in Glory*, the painting that won Tintoretto his commission. In the main hall are ceiling paintings (1575–81) describing episodes from the Old Testament, all carefully chosen to draw parallels with the *scuola*'s charitable or curative aims. The 10 wall paintings show scenes from the New Testament. Note the superb 17th-century wooden carvings around the walls, by the little-known sculptor Francesco Pianta. Of the eight paintings downstairs, the artist's last in the *scuola* (1583–88), the best are the idiosyncratic *Annunciation* and *The Flight into Egypt*.

THE BASICS

scuolagrandesanrocco.it

🔢 E5

✉ Campo San Rocco, San Polo 3052

☎ 041 523 4864

🕐 Daily 9.30–5.30

🍴 Campo dei Frari

🚊 San Tomà N, 1, 2

♿ Poor

💶 Expensive

❓ A leaflet about the *scuola*'s paintings is usually free with your ticket; audio guides are also available

24 Scuola di San Giorgio degli Schiavoni

HIGHLIGHTS

- *St. George Slaying the Dragon*
- *Triumph of St. George*
- *St. George Baptizing the Gentiles*
- *The Miracle of St. Tryphon*
- *The Agony in the Garden*
- *The Calling of St. Matthew*
- *The Vision of St. Augustine*

TIP

- Allow a while for your eyes to accustom to the dim light, and take time to pick out the detail in the paintings.

This intimate *scuola*, with its charming Carpaccio paintings, allows you the opportunity to look at works of art in the building for which they were painted, rather than in a gallery venue.

Slavs This tiny *scuola* (religious or charitable confraternity) was founded in 1451 to look after Venice's Dalmatian, or Slav (Schiavoni), population. Dalmatia, roughly modern Croatia, was one of the earliest territories absorbed by Venice, in the ninth century. In 1502, Vittore Carpaccio, famous for his St. Ursula cycle in the Gallerie dell'Accademia, was commissioned to decorate the humble *scuola* with scenes illustrating the lives of Dalmatia's three patron saints: St. George, St. Tryphon and St. Jerome. On their completion (in 1508), the paintings

Clockwise from left: Looking towards the scuola; *detail of* St. George Slaying the Dragon *by Carpaccio; stone fish detail on the exterior*

were installed in the headquarters' upper gallery and moved to their present position when the *scuola* was rebuilt in 1551.

Art cycle The nine-painting cycle starts on the north wall with *St. George Slaying the Dragon* (1502–08), while to its right is the *Triumph of St. George*, *St. George Baptizing the Gentiles* and *The Miracle of St. Tryphon*, which depicts the boy-saint exorcizing a demon from the Roman Emperor's daughter. Right of the altarpiece by Carpaccio's son, Benedetto, are *The Agony in the Garden* and *The Calling of St. Matthew*, followed by three works featuring St. Jerome, an early church father. The best known is the *Vision of St. Augustine*, with the saint in his study having a vision announcing Jerome's death.

HIGHLIGHTS

● Basilica di Santa Maria Assunta
● Santa Fosca church
● View from the campanile

The rural backwater of Torcello, in the far northeast of the lagoon, is Venice's most ancient settlement. It's the site of a superb basilica, the oldest building in Venice.

Seeing Torcello From the landing stage, a path runs beside Torcello's canal, crossed by the simple stone span of the Ponte del Diavolo (Devil's Bridge), to the main piazza. Grouped around here is everything there is to see. You will also find the so-called Trono di Attila, a primitive stone chair once used by the bishop.

Island churches One of the most magical places in Venice, Torcello was probably the city's birthplace and the first area of the lagoon to be settled in the fifth century. Malaria and the silting up of its canals snuffed out its prosperity

Clockwise from far left: The view from the bell tower across Torcello; candles inside Santa Fosca church; Madonna and Child mosaic in Santa Maria Assunta; a canal running through the farmland; exterior of Santa Fosca; a mosaic in Santa Maria Assunta depicting hell

in the 12th century, and today it is little more than a single hamlet and a beautiful patchwork of green fields and leafy canals. Torcello is dominated by the cathedral of Santa Maria Assunta. This is Venice's oldest building (founded 639) and one of its loveliest sights, as well as the finest Veneto-Byzantine church in Italy. The lofty interior, bare and cool, has some superb mosaics dating from the ninth to 12th centuries, on the vaults and walls. Climb the bell tower for wonderful lagoon views across the mudflats and marsh. Also worth seeing close by are the 11th-century Byzantine church of Santa Fosca and the small Museo dell'Estuario, which houses a low-key display of archaeological finds from Torcello and the lagoon. It's the perfect antidote to the crowds and heat of Venice.

THE BASICS

museotorcello.
servizimetropolitani.ve.it
🔡 See map ▷ 115
🚤 Line 12 from
Fondamente Nove to
Burano, then No. 9 boat to
Torcello, every 60–90 min,
takes 45 min. Get the earliest boat to avoid a crowd

Museo dell'Estuario
☎ 041 730 761
🕐 Mar–Oct daily 10.30–
5.30; Nov–Feb daily 10–5
💶 Inexpensive

Basilica di Santa Maria Assunta
☎ 041 730 761
🕐 Mar–Oct daily 10.30–6;
Nov–Mar daily 10–5
💶 Moderate; combined
ticket for museum, basilica
and bell tower expensive

More to See

This section contains other great places to visit if you have more time. Some are in the heart of the city while others are a short journey away, found under Farther Afield. This chapter also has fantastic suggestions for excursions for which you should set aside a whole day.

In the Heart of the City

ANGELO RAFFAELE

The ancient church of the Archangel Raphael was founded in the eighth century; the present Greek cross-shaped building, with its two bell towers, dates from the 17th. Well off the beaten track, its visitor numbers soared following the success of Salley Vickers' book *Miss Garnet's Angel*; the church plays a starring role in the novel. Above the main door stands a charming statue of the Angel, holding the hand of the boy Tobias, accompanied by a dog, and holding a fish, which plays a key role in the story. Inside, there are more reminders of the apocryphal story, with the stars of the show painted on the organ loft by Gianantonio Guardi.

➕ C6 ✉ Campo Angelo Raffaele, Dorsoduro 1721 🕐 Daily 9–12, 3–5 🚤 San Basilio 2, 8 🎟 Free

ARSENALE

The Arsenale, Venice's vast former shipyards, are now used for exhibitions during Venice's Biennale and for the annual Festival of Boats each May. Work on opening more areas, more frequently, is ongoing with a view to reinstating the entire area as a vibrant part of the city.

➕ M6 ✉ Campiello della Malvasia, Castello ☎ 041 270 9546 🚤 1, 4.1, 4.2 🎟 Varies with exhibition

CA' PESARO

capesaro.visitmuve.it

The Ca' Pesaro presents its best face to the Canal Grande, but its waterfront facade can also be glimpsed from the ends of several alleys off the Strada Nova. It was bought as three separate buildings in 1628 by the Pesaro family, who subsequently commissioned Baldassare Longhena, one of Venice's leading 17th-century architects, to unite the component parts behind one of the city's grandest baroque facades. Today it houses Venice's Galleria d'Arte, Galleria Internazionale d'Arte Moderna (Gallery of Modern Art) and the Museo d'Arte Orientale, displaying Chinese and Japanese art and objects.

Beautiful Ca' Pesaro houses galleries of modern and oriental art

G4 ✉ Canal Grande-Fondamenta Ca' Pesaro, Santa Croce 2070–76 ☎ 041 721127 🎫 Galleria and Museo Apr–Oct Tue–Sun 10.30–6; Nov–Mar Tue–Sun 10.30–4.30 🚤 San Stae N, 1 ♿ Poor 💶 Galleria and Museo expensive

CAMPO DEI MORI

This sleepy little square may take its name either from the Moorish merchants who traded on the *fondaco* nearby, or from three silk merchants—Robia, Sandi and Alfani Mastelli who settled in the Palazzo Mastelli north of the *campo*. In time, they may have inspired the *Mori* (Moors), three statues built into the walls of the piazza's houses. The building numbered 3399, along the Fondamenta to the east of the *campo*, was home to the painter Tintoretto between 1575 and his death in 1594.

G2 ✉ Campo dei Mori, Cannaregio 🚤 Orto 4.1, 4.2, 5.1, 5.2

CAMPO SANTA MARGHERITA

This may well become your favorite Venetian square, thanks mainly to its friendly and informal air, its collection of little bars and cafés, and its easy-going street life, which remind you that Venice is still a living city. It's busy with Venetians throughout the day, shopping at the market stalls in the morning, and meeting to chat and sip coffee in the afternoons while children play and dogs race round. Evenings see flocks of students from the nearby university drinking outside bars; Margaret Duchamp, on the corner, Il Caffè and Il Doge are all popular and have outside tables. The Scuola Grande di San Rocco (▷ 58), the Frari (▷ 48), and the Accademia (▷ 24) are within easy reach.

E6 ✉ Dorsoduro 🍴 Cafés 🚤 Ca' Rezzonico 1

GESUITI

This lofty, shadowy and incredibly ornate church, built by the Jesuits in 1715, is renowned for its extraordinary marble *trompe-l'œil*, best seen in the pulpit on the left, whose solid stone is carved to resemble pelmets, tassels and curtains of figured damask and

Informal Campo Santa Margherita

Tintoretto's house in Campo dei Mori

velvet. The church also boasts Titian's *Martyrdom of St. Lawrence* (in the first chapel on the left) and Tintoretto's *Assumption of the Virgin* (in the left transept).

➕ J3 ✉ Campo dei Gesuiti, Cannaregio 4885 ☎ 041 523 1610 🕐 Daily 10–12, 4–6/7 🚤 Fondamente Nove 4.1, 4.2, 5.1, 5.2 ♿ Good 🎫 Free

GIARDINI SAVORGNAN

Push open the iron gate on the Fondamenta Savorgnan on the Canale di Cannaregio and discover one of the area's best-kept secrets, the surprisingly spacious, tree-shaded Giardini Savorgan. Once the private garden of the *palazzo* standing on one side, this grassy space is a great place for a picnic or a breather.

➕ E3 ✉ Fondamenta Savorgnan, Cannaregio 3012 🚤 Guglie 4.1, 4.2, 5.1, 5.2 🎫 Free

GIARDINO PAPADOPOLI

The Giardino Papadopoli, once one of the largest private gardens in Venice, stands at the west end of the Canal Grande, a stone's throw from Piazzale Roma. It's a great place to wait for transportation to the mainland—you can reach the station across the Ponte della Costituzione, opened in 2007 to mark the new millennium. The gardens were laid out in 1810 when a group of buildings were demolished, including the church of Santa Croce, which gave its name to this *sestiere*.

➕ D4 ✉ Fondamenta Papadopoli, Santa Croce 🚤 Piazzale Roma 1, 2 🎫 Free

ISOLA DI SAN MICHELE

It's a short hop on the *vaporetto* to Venice's atmospheric cemetery island with its Renaissance church. Most of Isola di San Michele is covered by the cemetery, where Venetians are buried in tiers of stone coffin drawers or rest under an assortment of monuments. Don't miss the tombs of the composer Stravinsky and the impresario Serge Diaghilev.

➕ L1–L2 ✉ Isola di San Michele ☎ 041 729 2811 🕐 Apr–Sep daily 7.30–6; Oct–Mar daily 7.30–4; 25 Dec, 1 Jan 7.30–12 🚤 Cimitero 🎫 Free

Tulips blooming in Giardino Papadopoli

The cemetery on Isola di San Michele

MERCERIE

The *calli* between San Marco and Rialto are known as the Mercerie, once synonymous with luxury goods. Today, the shops sell everything from expensive high fashion to tourist kitsch.

🔂 H5 ⊠ San Marco 🚤 Rialto N, 1, 2, 4

MUSEO DELLA FONDAZIONE QUERINI STAMPALIA

querinistampalia.org

The Fondazione Querini Stampalia, housed in a Renaissance palazzo, promotes study and culture. Its modernized ground floor is an excellent example of the work of architect Carlo Scarpa. The museum is in the unchanged period rooms on the second floor, giving a real taste of an 18th-century palazzo. Stars of the show are Giovanni Bellini's superb *Presentation in the Temple* and two series of paintings: 67 studies of Venetian festivals by the 18th-century artist Gabriele Bella, and a collection of genre paintings by Pietro Longhi (1702–85) showing everyday Venetian life.

🔂 J5 ⊠ Campiello Querini Stampalia, Castello 5252 ☎ 041 271 1411 🕐 Tue–Sun 10–6 🚤 San Zaccaria, 1, 2, 4.2, 5.2 💷 Expensive

MUSEO STORICO NAVALE

The enjoyably presented displays of maritime ephemera here put Venice and the sea into a clear historical context.

🔂 M7 ⊠ Campo San Biagio, Castello 2148 ☎ 041 2424 🕐 Apr–Oct daily 10–6; Nov–Mar daily 10–5 🚤 Arsenale 1, 4.1, 4.2 ♿ Poor 💷 Moderate

PALAZZO CONTARINI DEL BOVOLO

gioiellinascostidivenezia.it

This Gothic palazzo is best known for its sinuous exterior staircase. Such staircases are called *scale a chiocciola* (snail stairs) in Italian, and the Venetian dialect for snail is *bovolo*. The beautiful redbrick and Istrian stone stairway gives access on five levels to graceful loggias curving around inside a tower.

🔂 G6 ⊠ Calle dei Risi, San Marco 🕐 Daily 10–6 🚤 Rialto N, 1, 2 ♿ None 💷 Moderate

Museo Storico Navale

The Geography Lesson by Pietro Longhi in Museo della Fondazione Querini Stampalia

PALAZZO GRASSI

palazzograssi.it

Outside, nothing could be more traditionally 18th-century classical than this palace. Inside, it's another story; the interior was converted in the 1980s by Gianni Agnelli of Fiat to become Venice's highest-profile exhibition venue. In 2004, after the death of Agnelli, it was bought by François Pinault, French millionaire collector and owner of a business empire that includes Gucci. It reopened in 2007 as a venue for temporary exhibitions, designed to be seen in conjunction with the collection at the Punta della Dogana (▷ 38–39) and centered on Pinault's own collection of 20th- and 21st-century contemporary art.

✚ F6 ✉ Campo San Samuele, San Marco 3231 ☎ 041 240 1308 🕲 Wed–Mon 10–7 🚤 Sant'Angelo 1, San Samuele 2 💰 Expensive

PALAZZO MOCENIGO

mocenigo.visitmuve.it

The Palazzo Mocenigo near San Stae is one of several palazzi in the city built by the Mocenigo family, among the grandest and oldest of the noble Venetian clans. The palace now houses a museum dedicated to textiles, costumes and perfume, which is worth a visit for a fascinating glimpse of 18th-century fashionable life. You can even mix your own scent in the Perfume Laboratoy.

✚ F4 ✉ Salizzada San Stae, Santa Croce 1992 ☎ 041 721 798 🕲 Apr–Oct Tue–Sun 10.30–5; Nov–Mar Tue–Sun 10.30–4.30 🚤 San Stae N, 1 💰 Moderate

PONTE DELL'ACCADEMIA

All the bridges across the Canal Grande have mesmerizing views, but none perhaps as lovely as those looking east from the Ponte dell'Accademia. There's been a bridge here since 1854; today's is the third version. It's identical in design to the Ponte degli Scalzi at the station, but built of wood, as stone was too expensive for construction across this much wider stretch of water.

✚ F7 ✉ Canal Grande, San Marco 🚤 Accademia N, 1, 2 ♿ Poor

Costume museum in the Palazzo Mocenigo

RIVA DEGLI SCHIAVONI

This broad quayside with its procession of palazzi, historic hotels, stalls and cafés, has great views, and is an ideal place for an evening stroll. It was named for the Slavic traders who brought cargo across the Adriatic.

🔲 K6–L6 ✉ Riva degli Schiavoni, San Marco to Castello 🚤 All services to San Zaccaria

SAN FRANCESCO DELLA VIGNA

This white church takes its name from a vineyard left to the Franciscans here in 1253. Many alterations have been made since, not least the facade, built by Palladio between 1562 and 1572. The best paintings are Antonio da Negroponte's *Madonna and Child* (1450), in the right transept, and Giovanni Bellini's *Madonna and Child* in the Cappella Santa, from where you can access the cloisters.

🔲 L5 ✉ Campo San Francesco, Castello 2786 ☎ 041 523 5341 🕐 Daily 8–12, 3–7 🚤 Celestia 4.1, 4.2, 5.1, 5.2 🚻 Good 💷 Free

SAN GIACOMO DELL'ORIO

chorusvenezia.org

Few Venetian buildings feel as old as San Giacomo, founded in the ninth century and added to over the years to produce an architectural hybrid. The 14th-century Gothic ship's-keel ceiling and the wooden Tuscan statue of the *Madonna and Child* are wonderful. There are superb paintings in the old and new sacristies and a high altarpiece, *Madonna and Child*, by Lorenzo Lotto.

🔲 F4 ✉ Campo San Giacomo dell'Orio, Santa Croce 1456 ☎ 041 275 0462 🕐 Mon–Sat 10.30–4.30 🚤 Riva di Biasio or San Stae 1 🚻 Good 💷 Inexpensive ❓ Chorus Group Pass and City Pass (▷ 4)

SAN GIOVANNI IN BRAGORA

Many people have a soft spot for San Giovanni in Bragora, the baptismal church of the Venetian composer Antonio Vivaldi.

Founded in the eighth century, it is one of Venice's oldest churches, its name deriving possibly from *brágora*, meaning "marketplace," or from two dialect words, *brago*

Riva degli Schiavoni

Interior decoration in San Francesco della Vigna

("mud") and *gora* ("stagnant canal"); from *bragolare* ("to fish"); or from the region in the Mideast that yielded the relics of St. John the Baptist, to whom the church is dedicated. Vivaldi was baptized here, and the original font, together with copies of his baptismal documents, are in the left nave.

The paintings in the lovely interior begin on the south wall to the left of the first chapel with a triptych by Francesco Bissolo and a *Madonna and Saints* by Bartolomeo Vivarini. Between these, above the confessional, stands a small Byzantine Madonna. A relief above the sacristy door is flanked on the left by Alvise Vivarini's *Risen Christ* (1498) and by Cima da Conegliano's *Constantine and St. Helena* (1502). Cima also painted the church's pictorial highlight, *The Baptism of Christ* (1494). On the wall of the left aisle is a small *Head of the Saviour* by Alvise Vivarini and Bartolomeo Vivarini's *Virgin Mary between John the Baptist and St. Andrew* (1478), to the right of the second chapel.

🔲 L6 ✉ Campo Bandiera e Moro, Castello 3790 ☎ 041 724 1044 🕐 Mon–Sat 9–12 🍴 Campo Bandiera e Moro 🚏 All services to San Zaccaria 🚻 Good 💶 Free

SAN MAURIZIO
artemusicavenezia.it
Rebuilt in the early 19th century and hardly used in the 20th, the church of San Maurizio found a new role in 2004 when it opened as the Museo della Musica. The chief draw is the fine collection of old musical instruments, whose sound provides the music that's a constant backdrop to your visit. You can buy CDs and DVDs relating to baroque music.

🔲 G6 ✉ Campo San Maurizio, San Marco ☎ 041 241 1840 🕐 Daily 10–7 🚏 Giglio 1 💶 Free

SAN NICOLÒ DEI MENDICOLI
San Nicolò was built in the 12th century and since 1966 it has been restored by the Venice in Peril Fund. The interior is superbly decorated with marbles,

The attractive interior of the church of San Giovanni in Bragora

statues, panels, paintings and gilded woodwork.

🚫 C6 ⊠ Campo San Nicolò dei Mendicoli, Dorsoduro 1907 ☎ 041 270 2464 ⓘ Mon–Sat 10–12, 4–6 🚢 San Basilio N, 2, 6, 8 ♿ Good 🎫 Free

SAN PANTALEONE

San Pantaleone is best known for its gargantuan ceiling painting, Gian Antonio Fumiani's *The Miracles and Martyrdom of St. Pantaleone* (1704). Smaller paintings include Veronese's touching piece *St. Pantaleone Healing a Boy* (1587; second chapel on the right).

🚫 E6 ⊠ Campo San Pantalon, San Polo 3765 ☎ 041 272 8611 ⓘ Mon, Wed, Fri, Sun 10–12.30, 3.30–6, Tue, Thu, Sat 10–12.30, 3.30–7 🚢 San Tomà 1, 2 ♿ Good 🎫 Free

SAN POLO

chorusvenezia.org

Founded in 837 but much altered since, the church of San Polo is renowned for Giandomenico Tiepolo's *Via Crucis*, or *The Stations of the Cross* (1747),

an 18-panel cycle of paintings in the sacristy. Tintoretto's turbulent *Last Supper* (1547) hangs on the west wall, while the apse chapel contains Veronese's *Marriage of the Virgin*.

🚫 F5 ⊠ Campo San Polo, San Polo 2102 ☎ 041 275 0462 ⓘ Mon–Sat 10.30–4.30 🚢 San Silvestro 1 ♿ Good 🎫 Inexpensive ❓ Chorus Group Pass and City Pass (▷ 4)

SAN ZACCARIA

Founded in the ninth century, the church of San Zaccaria has gone through several architectural overhauls down the centuries and is now a beguiling mix of Gothic and Renaissance style, beautifully articulated in the facade. The brickwork on the right dates from the 14th century, the upper marble-fronted elevation from 1481. Inside, there's a sublime *Madonna and Child with Saints* (1505) by Giovanni Bellini, an early Tintoretto, Renaissance frescoes by Andrea del Castagno and another altarpiece by Antonio Vivarini. Don't miss the distinctly water-logged

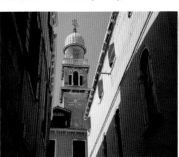

The view along a street to San Pantaleone

An exhibition in San Maurizio

crypt, the only one in Venice, and resting place of eight doges.

➕ K6 ✉ Campo Campo di San Zaccaria, Castello 4693 ☎ 041 522 1257 🕒 Mon–Sat 10–12, 4–6, Sun 4–6 🚤 San Zaccaria ♿ Good 🎟 Free; Cappella di San Tarasio inexpensive

SANTO STEFANO

chorusvenezia.org

Delight in the sensation of walking from the bustle of the city into a building that induces immediate calm, thanks to its soothing Gothic interior. One of Venice's loveliest churches, Santo Stefano is ideally placed at the edge of the charming Campo Santo Stefano (also known as Campo Francesco Morosini); nearby Paolin (▷ 150) is the perfect place to sit with a drink or ice cream.

The church has not always been so peaceful. It was reconsecrated six times to wash away the stain of blood spilled by murders within its walls. Today, its interior is over-arched by an exquisite ship's keel ceiling and framed by tie beams and pillars of Greek and red Veronese marble. In the middle of the nave lies Doge Francesco Morosini (d.1612, and buried under Venice's largest tomb slab). He was famous for recapturing the Peloponnese and blowing up the Parthenon with a single shot.

Other tombs, notably Pietro Lombardo's *Monument to Giacomo Surian* (d.1493) on the wall to the right of the main door, command attention, but the church's chief artistic interest lies in the gloomy sacristy at the end of the right nave. The altar wall displays two narrow-framed saints by Bartolomeo Vivarini, as well as a recessed 13th-century Byzantine icon. On the walls to either side are four paintings by Tintoretto and four portraits of Augustinian cardinals, displayed here as Santo Stefano is an Augustinian church.

➕ G6 ✉ Campo Santo Stefano (Campo Francesco Morosini), San Marco 2774 ☎ 041 275 0462 🕒 Mon–Sat 10.30–4.30 🍴 Campo Santo Stefano 🚤 San Samuele or Sant' Angelo N, 1, 2 ♿ Very good 🎟 Inexpensive ❓ Chorus Group Pass and City Pass (▷ 4)

The spacious Campo Santo Stefano

SQUERO DI SAN TROVASO

Venice had more than 10,000 gondolas in the 16th century; today there are only a few hundred, built in a handful of specialist boatyards *(squeri)*. One of the most famous, and easiest to see, is the Squero di San Trovaso, on the waterfront of the Rio San Trovaso, just behind the Zattere. Construction sheds and workshops are set back from the *rio*, and there's generally activity of some sort as gondolas are repaired. Modern water conditions take a toll on the boats, which suffer from the backwash of motorboats, and they need to be cleaned and overhauled as often as once a month. To get a real insight into the expertise of the gondolier, take a *traghetto* across the Canal Grande and watch the boatmen.

➕ E8 ✉ Rio San Trovaso, Dorsoduro
🚤 Zattere N, 2, 5.1, 6, 8, 10

TEATRO LA FENICE

teatrolafenice.it

Fenice is the Italian for phoenix, and Venice's opera house, designed by Giannantonio Selva in 1792, rose from the ashes of the disastrous fire of 1996 to reopen for the 2004–5 season. The new hall is a delight. You should book well in advance for performances or join one of the regular tours.

➕ G6 ✉ Campo San Fantin, San Marco 1965 ☎ Tickets and information 041 2424; guided tours and groups 041 786 672; festfenice.com 🕐 Daily with audio guides to fit around rehearsals; check with theater
🚤 Giglio 1 💰 Expensive

TORRE DELL'OROLOGIO

torreorologio.visitmuve.it

San Marco's clock tower was built between 1496 and 1506. The exterior stone dial shows the hours in Roman numerals; the interior face shows the signs of the zodiac and phases of the moon.

➕ J6 ✉ Piazza San Marco, San Marco 30124 ☎ Book online or tel 848 082 000 (from abroad 00 39 041 4273 0892); reservations compulsory 🕐 Guided visits in English Mon–Wed 11, 12, Thu–Sun 2, 3
🚤 San Marco Vallaresso, San Marco Giardinetti N, 1, 2 and all services to San Zaccaria 💰 Expensive

The auditorium, Teatro La Fenice

Torre dell'Orologio with its blue enameled clock

Farther Afield

BURANO

Tucked into the northeast of the lagoon, Burano combines its role as a functioning fishing community with that of a tourist honeypot, its charming canals and streets lined with brightly colored houses. It is also known for its lace making, and you can see superb examples at the Museo del Merletto; be aware, however, that much of the lace on sale in the souvenir shops is imported from Asia.

➕ a4–c5 ⊠ Isola di Burano 🚢 12 from Fondamente Nove, every 60–90 min

Museo del Merletto

➕ b5 ⊠ Piazza Galuppi 187 ☎ 041 730 034; museomerletto.visitmuve.it ⏰ Apr–Oct Tue–Sun 10.30–5; Nov–Mar Tue–Sun 10.30–4.30 💶 Moderate

THE LIDO

The Lido is essentially a long, narrow sandbank, once a sparsely inhabited island of dunes and pinewoods. Today it combines its role as a residential suburb with that of a seaside resort and overspill hotel area for Venice. A 10-minute boat trip from the city will bring you to a different world, where cars, buses and supermarkets are the backdrop to lazy beach days. More active pursuits include tennis and golf, as well as walking and cycling. You could also take in some of the Lido's superb art nouveau and art deco buildings, such as the Hotel Excelsior, a neo-Moorish fantasy.

➕ See map ▷ 115 🚢 Lido

SANT'ERASMO

Bigger than Venice itself, Sant'Erasmo is one of the lagoon's best-kept secrets. It lies northeast of the city, a long, flat, sparsely inhabited island where sandy paths crisscross neat fields and tiny vineyards. Sant'Erasmo produces huge quantities of vegetables for the city markets. The island is traversed by a single road, where rickety old unlicensed cars trundle up and down. The island does have a tiny store at the main settlement, built around the church, and a couple of *trattorie*.

➕ See map ▷ 115 ⊠ Isola di Sant'Erasmo 🚢 Capannone, Chiesa, Punta Vela 13 from Fondamente Nove

Rio Pontinello on Burano, lined with moored vessels and colorful houses

Excursions

CHIOGGIA

This excursion takes in the west end of the Lido and the island of Pellestrina en route to the ancient town of Chioggia.

Pellestrina is a contrast to the developed, bustling Lido, a sand-swept spit of land, bordered on the sea side by the *murazzi*, the sea defence walls erected in the 18th century. Its three main villages earn their living from fishing, both from the boats you'll see moored and from the floating huts just offshore.

Chioggia is a Roman foundation and one of the earliest settlements on the lagoon, a past reflected in its layout, a grid pattern of three straight streets intersected by canals. The main street, Corso del Popolo, is lined with old buildings and is home to the 14th-century *granaio* (grainstore), behind which is the *pescheria*, the fish market. Further along the Corso are the churches of Sant'Andrea Apostolo, San Jacopo and the Duomo (cathedral).

Past here, the Museo Civico della Laguna Sud is housed in a 15th-century Franciscan convent. It tells the story of Chioggia and the southern lagoon, with displays on the Roman epoch and a collection of boats and fishing artifacts on the upper floors.

From here, head east along the main Canale della Vena, an almost impossibly picturesque waterway with brightly painted fishing boats, tiny arcaded shops, fruit and vegetable stalls and flapping washing hanging up in the adjoining courtyards. The waterfront is the main food shopping street and thronged all morning, while the narrow *calli* leading off illustrate how the town has retained its medieval layout.

The church of San Domenico, standing on its own island at the lagoon end, was founded in the 13th century and contains the 1520 *St. Paul,* the last picture painted by Carpaccio.

Do try to include lunch while in Chioggia; the restaurants here are noted for their fish and seafood, and prices are lower than in Venice. You could stop on the way back to town for a swim at one of Pellestrina's quiet beaches or at the Lido itself.

Distance: From the Lido 25km (16 miles)
Journey time: 1 hour from the Lido
Transport: Co-ordinated bus and waterbus service; No. 11 bus from Lido, connect with *motonave* 11 to Chioggia from Pellestrina

Museo Civico della Laguna del Sud

✉ San Francesco Fuori le Mure, Campo Marconi, Chioggia ☎ 041 550 0911
🕐 Jun–Aug Tue–Wed 9–1, Thu–Sun 9–1, 9–11; Sep–May Tue–Sun 9–1
💰 Moderate

Bridge over the Canale della Vena

PADUA

turismopadova.it

Historic Padua is a university city and important economic center, where art, monuments, churches and shops are scattered around a compact, attractive center. Aim to arrive early, taking the tram from outside the station to the center.

The historic hub centers around the Palazzo della Ragione, medieval Padua's assembly hall and law courts, built between 1218 and 1219. The vast building has a remarkable cycle of 15th-century astrological frescoes in the main hall, which also contains a huge wooden horse, constructed for a tournament in 1466. The first floor has been home to food stalls for over 800 years, while the Piazza della Frutta and Piazza dell'Erbe, on each side of the palazzo, host one of northern Italy's most vibrant produce markets.

Near here is the splendidly eclectic Caffè Pedrocchi, whose upstairs rooms, the 19th-century hub of Padovan intellectual life, are decorated in every style from Egyptian and Etruscan to Renaissance. South of here, reached down Via del Santo, is the Basilica di Sant'Antonio, one of Italy's main pilgrim shrines, built between the mid-13th and 14th centuries and flanked by a superb equestrian bronze of Gattamelata by Donatello (1453).

Padua's main artistic site lies to the north, nearer the station, a complex including the Cappella degli Scrovegni, the Musei Civici Eremitani and the Palazzo Zuckermann. The Scrovegni chapel was built in 1300 by Enrico Scrovegni to atone for his father's usury. From 1303 to 1309 the walls were frescoed by Giotto with scenes from the life of Christ and the Virgin, set against a radiant blue background. Considered one of the turning points in Western art, the perspectival elements, the realistic details and expressions show a wholly innovative naturalism and fluency. The other parts of the complex showcase archaeology, sculpture, painting and the decorative and applied fine arts.

Palazzo della Ragione, Padua

Distance: 32km (20 miles)
Journey time: 25–35 min
Transport: Bologna line from Venezia Santa Lucia; SITA buses from Piazzale Roma
🚩 Stazione FS ☎ 049 520 7415
🕐 Mon–Sat 9–7, Sun 10–4
🚩 Galleria Pedrocchi ☎ 049 520 7415
🕐 Mon–Sat 9–7, Sun 10–4

Cappella degli Scrovegni

cappelladegliscrovegni.it
✉ Piazza Eremitani 8 ☎ 049 201 0020; book by phone or online 72 hours in advance, tickets to be collected 1 hour in advance 🕐 Daily 9–7 💶 Expensive

VICENZA

vicenzae.org

Cradled in green hills, beautiful Vicenza, with its glossy shops, smart restaurants and easy lifestyle, is famed for its palazzi and civic buildings, the work of the 16th-century's most influential architect, the great Andrea Palladio.

Dating from Roman times, the town stands on two rivers and became a Venetian possession in 1404. Its architectural makeover came in the 16th century, when Palladio and his neoclassical style burst upon the scene. Born in Padua, Palladio found his major patron, the humanist Trissino, in Vicenza and, between 1540 and 1580, transformed the city.

Vicenza is bisected by the Corso Palladio, lined with a procession of mansions and palazzi, no fewer than five designed by Palladio, while others are scattered throughout the city center. The Corso opens into Piazza Matteotti, home to both the Teatro Olimpico and the Palazzo Chiericati (1550), one of Palladio's most triumphant buildings, now housing the Museo Civico and its fine art collection. Teatro Olimpico, Europe's oldest indoor theater, was designed by Palladio in 1579 and opened in 1585. The architect died before it was complete, though the astonishing *trompe l'oeil* permanent stage set of a classical city was inspired by his designs.

South from here lies the Piazza dei Signori, the heart of the *centro storico*. The square is dominated by Palladio's Basilica, enclosing the earlier Gothic Palazzo della Ragione, and his Loggia del Capitaniato, flanked by the Monte di Pietà, Vicenza's 16th-century pawn shop.

Elsewhere you'll find the Palazzo Leoni Montanari, home to another museum, the Duomo (cathedral) and some interesting churches.

Outside Vicenza are two renowned Palladian villas, Villa Valmarana, nicknamed "Ai Nani" for the stone dwarfs on its wall, with superb frescoes by Tiepolo father and son, and Villa Capra Valmarana, or Rotonda (1567).

Distance: 74km (47 miles)
Journey time: 55 min
Transport: Trains from Venezia Santa Lucia
🛈 Piazza Matteotti 12 ☎ 044 499 4770
🕐 Daily 9–5.30

Teatro Olimpico
✉ Piazza Matteotti 11, 36100 Vicenza
☎ 044 496 4380 🕐 Sep–Jun Tue–Sun 9–5; Jul–Aug 9–6 💶 Expensive (combined ticket for all Vicenza sites)

Museo Civico–Pinacoteca
✉ Palazzo Chiericati, Piazza Matteotti 37–39
☎ 044 422 2811 🕐 Sep–Jun Tue–Sun 9–5; Jul–Aug 10–6 💶 Expensive (combined ticket)

An ariel view across Vicenza

City Tours

This section contains self-guided tours that will help you explore the sights in each of the city's districts. Each tour is designed to take a day, with a map pinpointing the recommended places along the way. There is a quick reference guide at the end of each tour, listing everything you need in that district, so you know exactly what's close by.

San Marco

The historic *sestiere* of San Marco, the true heart of the city, is packed with palazzi, churches, museums, shops and restaurants. It runs east of the Canal Grande, from the iconic Piazza San Marco west towards the Rialto and its famous bridge.

Morning
Start your day in the **Piazza San Marco** (▷ 36–37; right), taking in the rich interior of the basilica before the hordes of day visitors from the cruise boats and coaches arrive. Then take the elevator up the **Campanile** (▷ 36–37), from where you'll get a bird's-eye view of the city, its lagoon and the islands, the perfect way to get your Venetian bearings.

Mid-morning
Splash out on mid-morning coffee at one of the piazza's celebrated cafés, before you stroll across to the **Palazzo Ducale** (▷ 34–35). Here, in the vast and opulent chambers, you'll get an insight into the grandeur and riches of Venice at the height of its power. If you want to learn more, spend an hour in the **Museo Correr** (▷ 32–33) at the opposite end of the piazza.

Lunch
There's a huge choice of lunch possibilities between the piazza and the **Rialto** (▷ 40–41)—a good bet would be **Acquapazza** (▷ 144), where you can sit outside and enjoy the freshest of fish on Campo Sant'Angelo, one of the area's nicest *campi*.

Afternoon
Spend the afternoon wandering through the maze of streets and squares towards the Rialto and its bridge, perhaps visiting the **Teatro La Fenice** (▷ 75), taking in some contemporary art at **Palazzo Grassi** (▷ 70; left), or the lovely **Santo Stefano** (▷ 74). If you're flagging, use the *vaporetti* along the Canal Grande.

Mid-afternoon

It's time to browse the shops of San Marco, where you'll find everything from the cheapest souvenirs to serious *alta moda* (high fashion). Good areas to shop are along the **Mercerie** (▷ 69), around Campo San Bartolomeo at the **Rialto** (▷ 40–41; right), or go where the serious money spends its cash and head for Calle Vallaresso, around the church of San Moïse and along the Largo XXII Marzo, an area that's home to just about every top Italian designer you can name. There are plenty of souvenir stalls on the waterfront near San Marco, some selling sketches, prints and watercolors.

Evening

Aim to finish your stroll on Campo Santo Stefano, where you can have a drink or one of the best ice creams in town at **Paolin** (▷ 150).

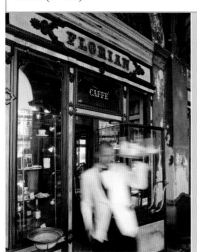

Dinner

Have dinner away from the piazza itself, but return later to see this wonderful space thronged with people and buzzing with conversation; not for nothing did Napoleon call it the "finest drawing room in Europe." Pull up a chair, listen to the music and sip a glass of Prosecco at **Caffè Florian** (▷ 147; left) or another of the piazza cafés.

Ca' d'Or

Palazzo
Mocenigo

Ca' Pesaro

Ca'
d'Oro

Ramo de la Vida

C del Savio

Campo
Nazario
Sauro

Ruga Vechia

Ruga Bella

San
Giacomo
dell' Orio

Campo San
Giacomo
dell'Orio

4

Campo dei
Tedeschi

Campo de
le Strope

Campo
Sant'Agostin

Campo
San
Boldo

Campo Santa
Maria Mater
Domini

Campo Santa
Maria Mater
Domini

Campo San
Cassan

Rio Marin
Fond. Rio Marin

Calle de la Laca

SAN
POLO

Campo
San Stin

Santa Maria
Gloriosa
dei Frari

5

Campo
dei Frari

San
Polo

Campo
San
Polo

San
Silvestro

Scuola
Grande
di San
Rocco

Campo
San Tomà

Campo de San
Silvestro

Canal
Grande

San
Angelo

6

Università
Ca' Foscari

San
Tomà

Teatrino di
Palazzo Grassi

Palazzo
Grassi

Campo
Sant'Anzolo

Ca'
Rezzonico

Ca' Rezzonico

San
Samuele

Campo
San Samuele

Santo
Stefano

San
Maurizio

Campo
Santo
Stefano

SA

Teatro
La Fenic

Campo
San Maurizio

Campo
Santa Maria
del Giglio

Rio Malpaga

Rio de la Toletta

Musica
A Palazzo

Santa Maria
del Giglio

7

Accademia

Ponte
dell'Accademia

Campo
San Vidal

Campo
Pisani

Canal   Grande

Gallerie
dell'Accademia

Campo San
Trovaso

Campo
San Vio

Collezione Peggy
Guggenheim

Squero di
San Trovaso

Campo
Sant'Agnese

Magazzini
del Sale

8

Zattere

Fondamenta Zattere ai Gesuati

E   **F**   **G**

85

San Marco Quick Reference Guide

Basilica di San Marco (▷ 14)

A superb 1,000-year-old church, rich in mosaics, whose architecture looks both to ancient Byzantium and medieval Europe. The treasures inside the building match its striking exterior. The altar is encrusted with precious gems.

Museo Correr (▷ 32)

Venice's city museum, telling the story of the historic Republic through sculpture, paintings, maps and artifacts. The paintings here represent Venice's finest artists. A hall is dedicated to sculptures by Antonio Canova.

Palazzo Ducale (▷ 34)

Once the seat of government and home to the Doge, this extraordinary palace is unique architecturally and artistically. Here you will find the largest oil painting in the world, by Tintoretto. The Bridge of Sighs is nearby.

Piazza San Marco and Campanile (▷ 36)

Venice's greatest square, lined with splendid buildings and arcades, is dominated by the detached Campanile with its views over the city and lagoon, and in fine weather to the Alps.

Rialto (▷ 40)

Once the commercial hub of the city, the Rialto bridge spans the Canal Grande, attracting locals and tourists to browse its wonderfully colorful fresh produce markets. Nearby streets house food shops.

CITY TOURS

Cannaregio

Venice's northwest *sestiere*, Cannaregio, one of the earliest areas to be developed, was, before the causeway and railway were built, the original entrance to the city. Full of contrasts, it sprawls from the station to the Rialto along the Canal Grande, an area that's busy and still densely populated by Venetians. To the north, things are quieter, and you'll find peaceful residential streets running between the wide *fondamente* (quaysides) that line a trio of parallel canals lying to the south of the open waters of the lagoon.

Morning
The **Canal Grande** (▷ 20–21) is at its most animated in the mornings, when it's bustling with *vaporetti*, delivery barges and flotillas of gondola tours. There are few better places to take in all this activity than from the portico of the upper floor of the **Ca' d'Oro** (▷ 16–17; right), so kick off your day by visiting this beautiful *palazzo* and its museum.

Mid-morning
You'll emerge to turn left on to the **Strada Nova**, a string of wide streets that connects the Rialto with the station and was created in the 19th century when numerous old houses were demolished. There's plenty of choice for a coffee break and the area is known for its good-value and wide range of shops. Turn right when you get to the Canale di Cannaregio and cut through to visit **Il Ghetto** (▷ 26–27). From here, head north, following the *fondamenta* along one of Cannaregio's wide canals.

Lunch
There's a choice of lunch spots along these canals; you could enjoy a delicious lunch of Venetian favorites with a modern twist at **Anice Stellato** (▷ 145; left) or take your time at the **Osteria l'Orto dei Mori** (▷ 149–150).

Afternoon

After lunch, cut through the **Campo dei Mori** (▷ 67) to visit the lovely church of **Madonna dell' Orto** (▷ 28–29; right). Then either walk or hop on the *vaporetto* to the Fondamenta Nuove, to take in the over-the-top delights of the sumptuous church of the **Gesuiti** (▷ 67–68).

Mid-afternoon

Follow the maze of streets south to **Santa Maria dei Miracoli** (▷ 50–51; left), one of the loveliest churches in Venice and a popular spot for weddings.

Evening

Enjoy a drink at an outside table, either in **Campo Santa Maria Nova**, right near the Miracoli and one of Venice's most underrated squares, or at a café in **Santi Apostoli**, always busy with locals and visitors.

Dinner

This part of Cannaregio has a good choice of restaurants and you couldn't do better than head for **Vini da Gigio** (▷ 151), which belongs to an association of restaurants that prides itself on serving genuine Venetian cuisine, with the accent on seasonal, fresh, traditional dishes. If you're up for more action, you could round off the evening by dropping into Venice's **Casino** (▷ 135), housed in the magnificent Palazzo Vendramin Calergi, right on the Canal Grande.

0   200 m

0   200 yds

Madonna
dell'Orto

Madonna
dell'Orto

*Sacca della
Misericordia*

Canale delle Fondamenta Nove

Museo di Fisica
Anton Maria
Traversi

Oratorio
dei Crociferi

Gesuiti

Fondamenta
Nove

Ca' d'Oro

Ca'
d'Oro

Campo
Santa
Sofia

Rialto
Mercato

Rio San

Campo Santi
Apostoli

Campiello
Riccardo
Selvatico

Campo San
Canzian

Campo dei
Miracoli

Santa Maria
dei Miracoli

Campo
Santi
Giovanni
e Paolo

Fondaco dei
Tedeschi

Teatro
Malibran

Campo
Santa
Marina

Borgoloco
Pompeo
Molmenti

Rialto

Campo San
Bartolomeo

Rialto

Campo San
Giacomo

Erbaria

Campo della
Pescaria

(H)

(J)

Cannaregio Quick Reference Guide

Ca' d'Oro (▷ 16)
Set directly on the Canal Grande, this medieval palazzo that belonged to the Contarini mercantile family is now an eclectic museum; its name, "House of Gold," comes from its original glittering facade.

Il Ghetto (▷ 26)
Established as the world's first Jewish ghetto in 1516, the Venetian Ghetto is set tucked away on its own island. In this thought-provoking enclave you can visit historic synagogues and a museum set in and around a beautiful campo.

Madonna dell'Orto (▷ 28)
Hidden in Venice's undiscovered northern fringes, this gem-like church was founded in 1350 and rebuilt in the Gothic style from 1399 to 1473. Later, Renaissance elements were added to the facade, while the interior is pure Gothic and ornamented with paintings by Tintoretto.

Santa Maria dei Miracoli (▷ 50)
Perfectly proportioned, this canalside Renaissance church was built in the 1480s in honor of a nearby miraculous shrine to the Virgin. Its beautiful polychrome marble exterior sets the tone for the light-filled interior, with its intricate and delicate carvings and sculpture.

CITY TOURS

Campo Santa Maria Nova, just across from Santa Maria dei Miracoli

Castello

Castello, the biggest Venetian *sestiere*, stretches from San Marco in the west to encompass the islands of San Pietro and Sant'Elena in the east. Historically, its shipbuilding Arsenale was the city's industrial heart, and is still surrounded by a vibrant working-class district. Its cityscape is varied, with a long southern waterfront, the Riva degli Schiavoni, overlooking St. Mark's Basin and a northern quayside that looks toward the main lagoon islands and the distant Alps.

Morning
Head first for **Campo Santa Maria Formosa**, where you can visit the church (▷ 46–47; right) and take in the art collection at the **Museo della Fondazione Querini Stampalia** (▷ 69) before exploring the surrounding *calli*, busy at this time of day with locals shopping. From here, head up to **Santi Giovanni e Paolo** (▷ 54–55) and its *campo*, now home to Venice's main hospital, housed behind the superb facade of what was once the Scuola Grande di San Marco.

Mid-morning
Emerging from the church, take a pause to enjoy a drink at one of the cafés surrounding the *campo*, before using your map to wend your way through the labyrinthine alleys to the serene Palladian church of **San Francesco della Vigna** (▷ 71). From here, follow the crowds southeast towards the **Arsenale** (▷ 66), a short hop from the **Museo Storico Navale** (▷ 69), where you can learn more about Venice's maritime history.

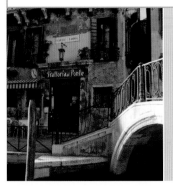

Lunch
There are plenty of lunch options here as you're back on the continuation of the **Riva degli Schiavoni** (▷ 71)—head for the good-value places on Via Garibaldi or cut though to **Da Remigio** (▷ 147) for a quintessentially Venetian eating experience at this traditional restaurant.

Afternoon

Now is the time to take in the glowing pictures in the **Scuola di San Giorgio degli Schiavoni** (▷ 60–61), before heading west to contrast this with the artistic treasures in **San Zaccaria** (▷ 73–74).

Mid-afternoon

You could relax now by taking the *vaporetto* to **Giardini**, an area of cool trees, benches and green open spaces, part of which is home to the permanent buildings used during Venice's annual Biennale art shows, showcasing art and architecture in alternate years.

Evening

Don't miss a pre-dinner drink on the waterfront (left), with views across St. Mark's Basin to the island of **San Giorgio Maggiore** (▷ 42–43).

Dinner

Castello has some of the best restaurants in Venice; try the long-established and renowned **Corte Sconta** (▷ 147; right), the superb **Osteria alle Testiere** (▷ 149) or the **Osteria Oliva Nera** (▷ 150), where you'll find the best of contemporary Venetian cooking.

Canale delle Fondamenta Nove

Ospedale

San Lazzaro
dei Mendicanti

Ospedale Santi
Giovanni e Paolo

Scuola Grande
di San Marco

Santi Giovanni
e Paolo

Santa Maria
dei Miracoli

Ospedaletto
(Santa Maria
dei Derelitti)

Teatro
Malibran

Rio de Santa Marina

Campo
Santa Marina

Borgoloco
Pompeo
Molmenti

CASTELLO

Campo
Santa
Maria
Formosa

Palazzo Grimani
di Santa Maria
Formosa

Campo
San Lorenzo

Santa Maria
Formosa

Museo della
Fondazione
Querini
Stampalia

Borgoloco San Lorenzo

Scuola di
San Giorgio
degli Schiavoni

Campo San
Zuane Novo

San
Zaccaria

Basilica di
San Marco

Museo
Diocesano

Campo San
Zaccaria

Piazza
San Marco

Museo
Correr

Campanile
Piazzetta
San Marco

Ponte
dei Sospiri

Riva degli
Schiavoni

Caffè
Florian

Museo
Archeologico

Palazzo
Ducale

Riva degli
Schiavoni

San
Zaccaria

San
Zaccaria

Riva degli
Schiavoni

San
Zaccaria
Pietà

Biblioteca
Nazionale
Marciana

Molo de Palazzo Ducale

Giardini Reali
di Venezia

Fondamenta dei Giardini

San Marco

San Marco

H   J   K

San Francesco della Vigna

Celestia

F. Case Nuove

Campo San Francesco

Corte e Ponte

Calle del Cimitero

Campo della Celestia

Rio di San Francesco

Salizada Santa Giustina

e Nova

C Sacca

Campo Santa Ternita

Rio della Celestia

Giardini dell'Ordine di Malta

del Furlani

Campo delle Cale

Campo Do Pozzi

Darsena Arsenale Vecchio

Rio dei Scudi Santa Ternita

Canale delle Galeazze

Darsena Grande

Calle de Tarco

Martin

Arsenale

Campo de l'Arsenal

San Giovanni in Bragora

Erizzo

Campo Bandiera e Moro

Calle Crotti

Calle Erizzo

Calle de la Vida

Schiavoni

Riva de Ca' di Dio

Fondamenta de l'Arsenal

Campo de la Tana

Ramo de la Tana

Museo Storico Navale

Arsenale

Campo San Biasio

Riva San Biasio

San Biagio

Rio de la Tana

Fondamenta de la Tana

Fondamenta de la Tana

Calle San

Calle del Forno

Via Giuseppe Garibaldi

la Marinaressa

Riva dei Sette Martiri

Monumento a Garibaldi

Canale di San Marco

Viale Giuseppe Garibaldi

Calle San Domenico

0   200 m
0   200 yds

Ⓛ   Ⓜ   Ⓝ

Castello Quick Reference Guide

TOP 25 SIGHTS AND EXPERIENCES

Santa Maria Formosa (▷ 46)
This interesting church and its *campo* are quintessentially Venetian—diverse architecture set about a lively square that, with its cafés and morning food stalls, is the hub of the neighborhood. The Byzantine 11th-century church was altered in 1492 in the new Renaissance style by Mauro Codussi and is full of treasures, while across the *campo* you'll find the Museo della Fondazione Querini Stampalia, one of the city's most beguiling museums.

Santi Giovanni e Paolo (▷ 54)
This huge Gothic preaching church is typical of those built by the mendicant religious orders, with a cavernous interior designed to accommodate large crowds. The *campo* it stands on showcases the superb facade of Venice's hospital, once a *scuola grande,* and an ebullient equestrian statue.

Scuola di San Giorgio degli Schiavoni (▷ 60)
Tucked away on a side canal, this charitable *scuola* is home to some of the most charming paintings in the city, a cycle by Carpaccio, painted in the first decade of the 16th century. You'll recognize St. George slaying the dragon while the terrified princess looks on.

Sunrise over the Riva degli Schiavoni

San Polo and Santa Croce

Enclosed by a loop of the upper stretches of the Canal Grande, the west-bank *sestieri* of San Polo and Santa Croce are densely populated, workaday districts, where there's a tangible sense of Venice as a living city. The Rialto, with its superb fish and fruit and vegetable markets, is the focus, with the big sights mainly lying south of here, among them fine churches and museums, while the whole area has good shopping and great bars and restaurants.

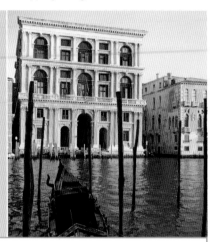

Morning
Start your day—and miss the worst of the crowds—by taking the *vaporetto* along the **Canal Grande** (▷ 20–21; right), alighting at San Tomà, the nearest stop to the great church of **Santa Maria Gloriosa dei Frari** (▷ 48–49), where you'll find plenty to fill in 40 minutes or so.

Mid-morning
You'll find good choices for a mid-morning stop on the Campo dei Frari—try **Bottega del Caffè Dersut** (▷ 146), where there are delicious smoothies, as well as excellent coffee, on offer. Then stroll round the side of the Frari to take in the mind-blowing architecture, incredible interior decoration and superb paintings by Tintoretto in the **Scuola Grande di San Rocco** (▷ 58–59).

Lunch
You could follow the main route up towards the Rialto and sit beside the Canal Grande for lunch at **Bancogiro** (▷ 146; left), where there's a choice of *cichetti* (Venetian-style tapas) as well as a full menu. Alternatively, choose somewhere in Campo San Polo, Venice's second largest square.

Afternoon

After lunch, you'll want to browse the stalls around the **Rialto bridge** (▷ 40–41), a good trawling ground for gifts and souvenirs. Later, take the *vaporetto* towards Piazzale Roma from Rialto Mercato, and get off at San Stae, from where you can visit two important museums, **Ca' Pesaro** (▷ 66–67), a magnificent palazzo housing the city's modern art collection, or **Palazzo Mocenigo** (▷ 70; left), home to a fascinating collection of costumes displayed in a great palace.

Mid-afternoon

From Palazzo Mocenigo it's a short stroll to **San Giacomo dell'Orio** (▷ 71; right), a fascinating church on a *campo* that's a good place to sit and relax with a drink. Explore the little streets around here, where you'll find tiny specialist shops and hidden corners.

Evening

If you haven't already taken it in, you can cut through from here to Campo San Polo to take in the church of **San Polo** (▷ 73) before joining the locals who congregate here for the early evening *passeggiata*.

Dinner

There's a great choice of restaurants to suit all tastes and pockets in the area—go upmarket and enjoy stunning modern cuisine at the **Antiche Carampane** (▷ 146), head for **Alla Madonna** (▷ 144), one of Venice's most famous and traditional fish restaurants, or enjoy an excellent pizza at **Il Refolo** (▷ 150), back on Campo San Giacomo dell'Orio.

0   200 m

0   200 yds

Guglie

Corte del Pielà

C del Pielà

Corte dei Muti

Calle del Riello

Fond dei Cannaregio

Corte del Savorgnan

Fondamenta Savorgnan

Giardini Savorgnan

Campo San Geremia

Corte de le Case Nove

C de la Chiesa

Calle Priuli dei Cavaletti

Fondamenta Sta Lucia

Calle Saffo

Calle de la Misericordia

Corte del Pozzo

PONTE DEGLI SCALZI

STAZIONE VENEZIA SANTA LUCIA

Ferrovia

Fond del Scalzi

Ferrovia

Ferrovia

Ferrovia

Campo San Simeon Grando

Riva de Biasio

Riva de Biasio

Fondamenta San Simeon Piccolo

C del Fenili

C San Simon Piccolo

Calle Nova di San Simon

Campo Santo

Fond de la Croce

Campo Nazario Sauro

Ruga Vechia

Campo dei Tedeschi

Ruga Bella

Campo Giacomo dell'Orio

Campo de le Strope

PONTE DELLA COSTITUZIONE

Piazzale Roma

STAZIONE AUTOBUS

Piazzale Roma

Giardino Papadopoli

Calle de le Case Nove

Calle de la Lana

Campo de la Lana

Rio de San Giovanni Evangelista

Calle de la Laca

Calle de la Laca

Rio Terà San Tomà

Fond Cont

Campo San Stin

SANTA CROCE

San Nicolo da Tolentino

Campo dei Amai

Campo dei Tolentini

Museo Leonardo da Vinci

Campo San Rocco

Scuola Grande di San Rocco

Santa Maria Gloriosa dei Frari

Campo dei Frari

Fondamenta Minotto

Fondamenta del Gaffaro

San Pantaleone

Campo San Pantalon

Rio delle Muneghette

Calle del Forno

Calle del Basegò

Calle del Basegò

Fondamenta Pagan

Fondamenta dei Tre Ponti

Fondamenta del Passamonte

Fondamenta delle Procuratie

Calle Contarini

Rio de Ca' Foscari

Università Ca' Foscari

Campo Santa Margherita

Scuola Grande dei Carmini

Campo dei Carmini

DORSODURO

Fondamenta Foscari

Rio di Santa Margarita

Palazzo Grassi

Ca' Rezzonico

Ca' Rezzonico

Calle del Traghetto

Rio Malpaga

Museo
di Fisica
Anton Maria
Traversi

Campo San
Marcuola

San Marcuola
Casinò

Musco di
Storia
Naturale di
Venezia

San
Stae

Campo
San Stae

Canal

Ca'
Pesaro

Ca' d'Oro

Grande

Palazzo
Mocenigo

Ca'
d'Oro

Campo
Santa
Sofia

an
Giacomo
dell' Orio

Campo
San
Boldo

Campo Santa
Maria Mater
Domini

Campo San
Cassan

Campo della
Pescaria

Rialto
Mercato

Campo
Sant'
Agostin

Erbaria

Campo San
Giacomo

SAN
POLO

Corte
Amaltea

Campo
San
Polo

Rialto

San
Polo

Rialto

San
Silvestro

Campo
de San
Silvestro

Teatro
Goldoni

Canal

Grande

Mercerie

San
Angelo

Campiello
de la Chiesa

Campo
San Luca

Campo
Daniele
Manin

Palazzo
Contarini
del Bovolo

San
Toma'

Teatrino di
alazzo Grassi

Campo
Sant'Anzolo

Santo
Stefano

San
Maurizio

Corte
Malatin

SAN MARCO

Campo
Santo
Stefano

Teatro
La Fenice

Campo
San Maurizio

San Polo and Santa Croce
Quick Reference Guide

Canal Grande (▷ 20)

If you do nothing else in Venice, take a *vaporetto* trip down this iconic waterway, which winds for 4km (2.5 miles) from Piazzale Roma to the glories of San Marco, with a spectacular pageant of some of the world's most beautiful buildings rising from the water on either side. Crossed by four bridges, the canal is lined with palazzi and churches whose architecture spans many styles.

Santa Maria Gloriosa dei Frari (▷ 48)

This impressive church, dating from the 13th century, was built for the Franciscans. Completed around 1395, the lofty interior contains masterpieces by some of Venice's greatest artists. Don't miss Titian's *Assumption of the Virgin* over the high altar, his *Madonna di Ca' Pesaro* in the left aisle, or Giovanni Bellini's triptych of the *Madonna and Child* in the sacristy.

Scuola Grande di San Rocco (▷ 58)

This headquarters of a charitable institution, or *scuola,* built between 1515 and 1549, was designed by Bartolomeow Bon. The interior is the perfect backdrop for the mind-blowing pictures by Tintoretto. His 54 paintings, on two floors, are one of the world's most impressive picture cycles by a single artist. Other works are by Titian, Giorgione, Bellini and Tiepolo.

CITY TOURS

CITY TOURS

Dorsoduro

Lying to the southwest of the Canal Grande, Dorsoduro's name means "hard back," referring to the firm land on which it stands. Its southern boundary is the Giudecca canal, edged by the long stretch of the sunny Zattere, its hub, lovely Campo Santa Margherita. It's a compelling *sestiere*, with three important galleries, superb churches, palazzi and *campi*, while the university lends a buzz and ensures good shopping, lively bars and a choice of restaurants.

Morning

You could start your day early with an overview of Venetian painting by taking in the **Gallerie dell'Accademia** (▷ 24–25). Be sure to climb the steps of the **Ponte dell'Accademia** (▷ 70; right) for one of the finest of all Venetian views, down the Canal Grande towards Santa Maria della Salute.

Mid-morning

Wend your way eastward through picturesque *calli* and *campi* to the **Collezione Peggy Guggenheim** (▷ 22–23), where you could have a drink at the excellent café before taking in the palazzo and art collections. From here, it's a short walk to the **Punta della Dogana** (▷ 38–39; left) and the church of **Santa Maria della Salute** (▷ 52–53).

Lunch

From Santa Maria della Salute it's a pleasant stroll along the Zattere, where there are plenty of lunch choices. Turn off at Rio San Trovaso for the **Cantina del Vino Già Schiavi** with its fine range of *cichetti* (a Venetian version of tapas), or sit and eat a pizza or simple lunch at one of the terrace restaurants on the Zattere itself.

Afternoon

Head back to **Ca' Rezzonico** (▷ 18–19) for a taste of hedonistic 18th-century interior design, before an afternoon trawling the charming backstreets of Dorsoduro. You could head to **San Sebastiano** (▷ 44–45; left), with its great Veronese paintings, or take in the lower-key charms of the contrasting churches of **San Nicolò dei Mendicoli** (▷ 72–73) or the **Angelo Raffaele** (▷ 66).

Mid-afternoon

Aim to finish your stroll by heading past the **Squero di San Trovaso** (▷ 75) to the Zattere, where you can buy one of the city's best ice creams at **Nico** (▷ 149), to enjoy on a bench looking across to the Giudecca.

Evening

Hit the tempting shops, to buy or browse, before heading to **Campo Santa Margherita** (▷ 67; left) where you can sit with a drink outside **Orange** (▷ 137), or one of the other bars, and soak up the atmosphere of this most appealing *campo*.

Dinner

Dorsoduro has restaurants for every taste and pocket, but among the nicest is **Antica Locanda Montin** (▷ 145), a long-established restaurant with a beautiful garden, which specializes in traditional Venetian cuisine. Then it's time for a nightcap—the **Zattere** is lovely at night with the lights of the Giudecca twinkling across the water.

Map Labels

4

PONTE DELLA
COSTITUZIONE
Piazzale
Roma

*Giardino
Papadopoli*

Autorimessa
Piazzale
Roma

STAZIONE
AUTOBUS

Piazzale
Roma

5

San Nicolò
da Tolentino
**SANTA
CROCE**

Museo
Leonardo
da Vinci

**Santa Mari
Glorios
dei Frar**

**Scuola
Grande
di San Rocco**

**San
Pantaleone**

Univer
Ca' Fos

6

**Campo
Santa
Margherita**

**Scuola
Grande
dei Carmini**

**Ca'
Rezzonico**

DORSODURO

**San Nicolò
dei Mendicoli**

**Angelo
Raffaele**

**San
Sebastiano**

Ospedale
Giustinian

7

Terminal
San Basilio

San Basilio

**Squero di
San Trovaso**

Zattere

8

GIUDECCA

Palanca

9

C   D   E

Dorsoduro Quick Reference Guide

 SIGHTS AND EXPERIENCES

Ca' Rezzonico (▷ 18)
Come to this magnificently opulent palazzo for a glimpse of the lifestyle of the 18th-century Venetian nobility.

Collezione Peggy Guggenheim (▷ 22)
Get an overview of all the main artistic movements of the second half of the 20th century.

Gallerie dell'Accademia (▷ 24)
An intimate gallery that takes you through the development of Venetian painting and showcases the work of the greatest painters.

Punta della Dogana (▷ 38)
This stunningly restored building, the best of 21st-century design, is home to changing exhibitions of cutting-edge contemporary art.

San Sebastiano (▷ 44)
This church is essentially a shrine to the great painter Veronese, who decorated virtually the entire interior.

Santa Maria della Salute (▷ 52)
This landmark church was built in the 18th century following an outbreak of the plague in Venice.

Scuola Grande dei Carmini (▷ 56)
See some of Tiepolo's best work in this intimate setting, designed by Baldassare Longhena.

Farther Afield

Venice's lagoon, 50km (31 miles) long, is scattered with numerous other islands, and most visitors spend time exploring at least some of them. These two itineraries explore the best, and both will need forward planning as *vaporetti* run less frequently to outlying areas.

DAY 1
Morning
Start your day with a visit to **Murano** (▷ 30–31; right), taking the No. 3 from Piazzale Roma or Ferrovia, or a boat from the Fondamente Nove. If you take this route, you could hop off for a short visit to the fascinating cemetery island of **San Michele** (▷ 60). On Murano, be sure to visit one of the glass factories, where you can watch glass-blowers at work, or visit the **Museo del Vetro** (▷ 31) to learn more. Then take the No. 12 *vaporetto* from the Faro stop for the 40-minute journey to **Burano** (▷ 76).

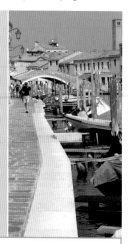

Lunch
Burano has good choices for lunch; try **Da Romano** (tel 041 730 030) or **Al Gatto Nero** (tel 041 730 120), both renowned for fish. After lunch, take a stroll round Burano, perhaps stopping off at the **Museo del Merletto** (▷ 76).

Afternoon
Back at the *vaporetto* stop, catch the No. 9 service for the short hop to **Torcello** (▷ 62–63), where you can visit the **Basilica di Santa Maria Assunta** (▷ 63; left) and church of **Santa Fosca** (▷ 63). You'll have to take the 9 line back to Burano to return to Venice.

Evening
The nicest route back to the city in summer is the No. 14 via Treporti and Punta Sabbioni, which gives you a chance to see more of the lagoon en route to the Lido. Change *vaporetti* here to return to Venice, either before or after dinner.

DAY 2
Morning
Catch *vaporetto* No. 2 to **San Giorgio Maggiore** (▷ 42–43; left) to visit Palladio's superb church, starting by taking the lift up the campanile for views over Venice and the lagoon islands. From June to mid-September, the No. 2 runs from San Giorgio to the **Lido** (▷ 76), where you're heading next. During other months, you'll have to return to San Zaccaria and change to the No. 1.

Lunch
Once on the Lido, there are plenty of choices for lunch on and just off the Gran Viale, which runs across the island from the lagoon to the Adriatic. The Lido's **beaches** are a big draw; some have private facilities and are ticket only, but others are free, so you could have a swim and a couple of hours on the beach if the weather's good.

Afternoon
Alternatively, take the 5.1 to the Fondamente Nove, where you connect with the No. 13 to the island of **Sant'Erasmo** (▷ 76; right). Here, you can walk for miles through vegetable fields and beside the lagoon. Disembark either at Capannone—if you want a good long walk—or Chiesa, and simply follow your nose along the island to eventually catch the boat back to Venice from the Punta Vela stop.

Mestre

Bissuola

Favaro Veneto

Tessera

A57

SR14 VIA MARTIRI DELLA LIBERTÀ

SS14 VIA ORLANDA

Canale Osellino

Campalto

Stazione
Venezia Mestre

VIA DELLA LIBERTÀ

Marghera

Parco San
Giuliano

Laguna di

Campalto

PONTE DELLA LIBERTÀ

San
Secondo

Stazione
Venezia
Santa Lucia

VENEZIA

Canale della Giudec

Giudecca

Bondante di Sotto

SP23

Fusina

San
Clemente

Sacca
Sessola

V
e
n
e
z
i
a

Santo
Spirito

Poveglia

L
a
g
u
n
a
d
i

Alberoni

Igoumenitsa,
Patras

Aeroporto
Marco Polo

Torcello

Mazzorbetto

Mazzorbo

Burano

V e n e z i a

Treporti

Murano

Lazzaretto
Nuovo

Sant'
Erasmo

Ca' Sávio

Isola di
San Michele

Isola del
Bacan

Punta
Sabbioni

Le
Vignole

La
Certosa

Canale di San Nicolò

San Giorgio
Maggiore

Isola di
Sant'Elena

Canale di San Marco

La
Grazia

San
Servolo

Lido

Porto
di Lido

San
Lazzaro

Lazzaretto
Vecchio

Lido

Piran,
Pula,
Poreč,
Rovinj,
Umag

Malamocco

Golfo   di

Venezia

| 0 | | 4 km |
| 0 | | 2 miles |

25 SIGHTS AND EXPERIENCES

Murano (▷ 30)

Ten minutes by *vaporetto* from Venice, the island of Murano, complete with its own canals, churches and palazzi, has been the center of Venetian glass manufacture since the Middle Ages. The Museo del Vetro tells the story and you can watch glass-blowing in the workshops. The beautiful 12th-century church of Santa Maria e Donato is another highlight.

San Giorgio Maggiore (▷ 42)

Across the Bacino di San Marco from the Palazzo Ducale, the little island of San Giorgio Maggiore (opposite) is dominated by the great Palladian church of the same name and its adjoining monastic buildings. Built between 1565 and 1610, the classical design shines with white marble and stucco, while the view from the campanile is one of Venice's finest.

Torcello (▷ 62)

More than an hour's journey from the city, in the far reaches of the northern lagoon, once heavily populated Torcello is home to an exquisite ninth-century Basilica, the oldest complete building in Venice, famous for its superb Byzantine mosaics. The island is also home to the church of 11th-century Santa Fosca and a small museum.

MORE TO SEE	**64**

Burano

Isola di San Michele

The Lido

Sant'Erasmo

Shop

Whether you're looking for the best local products, a department store or a quirky boutique, you'll find them all in Venice. In this section, shops are listed alphabetically.

SHOPS

Introduction

Venice was one of the world's greatest trading hubs for 500 years before its decline in the 17th century. Sumptuous goods from all corners of the globe filled its markets, shops and warehouses. Today, its trade is less exotic but still as tempting.

On Offer

Venice is a provincial city and its shops reflect this, though you'll find many designer names and some great Italian fashion, accessories and shoes. Transportation costs and high rents also mean prices are often higher than elsewhere.

Traditional Gifts

Venice's extraordinary history has bequeathed the city several unique shopping possibilities. The artisan traditions of Murano and Burano, for example, make glass and lace from these two lagoon islands good buys—though you must be on your guard against inferior, foreign-produced products. Glass trinkets can also provide some of Venice's most kitsch souvenirs.

Beautiful Masks

With the revival of the Venice carnival in 1979, the last few years has seen a proliferation of shops selling and producing the traditional masks (*maschere*) worn by celebrants. Some masks are mass-produced—but often still beautiful—while others are painstakingly

BURANO LACE

Although lace was made by women of all classes during the Middle Ages, it was the development of an intricate stitch known as Burano point that made the eponymous island (▷ 76) famous for its lace. Mass production in the 19th century devastated the industry, and today only a handful of women make lace by hand. Much of what you see for sale in Burano and the rest of Venice is foreign- or machine-made. For the real thing you will have to search long and hard and be prepared to pay high prices.

Clockwise from top: Masks hanging outside a shop; lace parasols in Burano; the Rialto fish market; a shop window display of Murano glass; hand-printed paper in

created by hand in workshops, such as Tragicomica (▷ 129) around the city. Locally produced masks are expensive, but they do make the most wonderful souvenirs.

Stationery Delights

Marbled paper, another traditional Venetian craft, has also enjoyed a revival since the 1970s and shops across the city sell a range of paper products. The craft is almost 1,000 years old, and spread from Japan to Persia and the Arab world during the Middle Ages. It reached Europe in about the 15th century. Mass-produced papers are perfectly good, but the best buys are authentic, made using old hand- and woodblock-printing techniques.

Delicate Materials

Shops selling a host of fine silks, damasks and other fabrics reflect the city's trading days. And, as you'd expect in a city with such an illustrious artistic past, there are many antiques shops filled with beautiful paintings, prints and *objets d'art* (▷ panel, 125).

And to Eat

Food souvenirs include pasta in every shape and form, rice and polenta, olive oil, dried *porcini* (mushrooms), vinegars, spices and traditional Burano biscuits.

MURANO GLASS

Glass-making began in Venice in Roman times, but took off in the 13th century, when foundries were moved to Murano (▷ 30–31) to lessen the risk of fire. Today, the island is a key production area; though shops sell Murano glass everywhere in Venice, the best choice, and keenest prices, are on the island. With its ornate forms and many tints, Murano glass is an acquired taste but the huge variety of styles includes both contemporary and traditional designs. At its best, glass is one of the city's most distinctive buys.

a range of designs; the view from the Rialto bridge toward Campo San Bartolomeo

Directory

ALIANI GASTRONOMIA

Perhaps Venice's most famous delicatessen, this shop has a superlative selection of cheeses, and a variety of hams, salamis, fresh pasta and other ready-made delicacies—all perfect for a picnic.

➕ G5 ✉ Ruga Vecchia San Giovanni, San Polo 654 ☎ 041 522 4913 🚤 Rialto or San Silvestro N, 1, 2

ANTICLEA ANTIQUARIATO

This beautiful little shop has a wonderful collection of antique Venetian beads and jewelry. The owner has spent a lifetime amassing her stock, the best of which is kept in countless small drawers around the walls. Beads of your choice can be made up, while you wait, into earrings or necklaces.

➕ K6 ✉ Campo San Provolo, Castello 4719/A ☎ 041 528 6946 🚤 San Zaccaria 1, 2, 4.1, 4.2, 5.1, 5.2

BAC ART STUDIO

bacart.com

For some stunning photos of Venice to take home and prove to people that it really does look dreamlike, Bac Art Studio has an impressive range. There are also framed prints of original art, as well as ceramics, porcelain, glass, stationery and calendars.

➕ F6 ✉ Calle delle Botteghe, San Marco 3451 ☎ 041 241 2898 🚤 San Samuele 2

BALLARIN

This excellent *pasticceria* has a superb range of cakes and pastries, to sample with a cup of coffee or take out. It also makes delicious chocolates and sweets— try the chocolate-coated orange peel, candied fruit or fresh cream chocolate truffles.

➕ H4 ✉ Salizzada San Giovanni Crisostomo, Cannaregio 5794 ☎ 041 528 5273 🚤 Rialto N, 1, 2

BARBIERI ARABESQUE

barbieriarabesque.com

This elegant shop sells nothing but scarves, stoles and pashminas in silk, wool and cashmere in a great range of hues and styles; all tracked down by the English-speaking owner, who has excellent contacts in the silk-weaving towns

Confectionery in a shop window on Campo San Luca

around Lake Garda. There are also scarves for dressing up, keeping you warm and adding individuality and luxury to any outfit.

🚩 K6 ☒ Ponte dei Greci, Castello 3403 ☎ 041 522 8177 ⛴ San Zaccaria 1, 2, 4.1, 4.2, 5.1, 5.2

BARENA
storevenezia.com

This understated and classy store sells beautifully tailored clothes for both men and women, but is most noted for its cloaks: the *tabarro* is a traditional draped cloak worn through the centuries by Venetians, and is warm, practical and elegant.

🚩 G6 ☒ Calle Minelli, San Marco 426/B ☎ 041 523 8457 ⛴ Sant'Angelo 1

CAMPO MARZIO
campomarzio.it

Campo Marzio stores specialize in brilliantly colored leather goods, with a particular emphasis on writing and desk accessories, especially beautiful pens. Styles range from classic to funky, and you'll find carrying cases for writing papers, documents and even headphones, while the braided leather key rings make great gifts.

🚩 G6 ☒ Calle della Mandola, San Marco 3546/a ☎ 041 522 0508 ⛴ Sant'Angelo 2

CASA DEL PARMIGIANO
aliani-casadelparmigiano.it

A stone's-throw from the Rialto markets, this delightful little family-run shop sells superb cheese (and not just Parmesan), a huge range of *salumeria* (delicatessen) from all over Italy and light-as-a-feather fresh homemade pasta. Locals consider this to be one of the best shops for gastronomic specialties in Venice, so be prepared to stand in line.

🚩 H5 ☒ Erberia, San Polo 214–15 ☎ 041 520 6525 ⛴ Rialto N, 1, 2

CLAUDIA CANESTRELLI

This tiny shop sells old prints, ornaments and lamps, but its chief draw is the beautiful 18th-century-style drop earrings made by the owner. Decorated with pearls, tiny rubies and emeralds, they are surprisingly good value.

🚩 G7 ☒ Campiello Barbaro, Dorsoduro 364/A ☎ 041 522 7072 ⛴ Accademia 1, 2 or Salute 1

COLORCASA

This shop is crammed with some of the most sumptuous decorating fabrics you can imagine—silks, brocades and figured velvets are for sale by the length or made up into cushions, drapes and bags. Silk key tassels and curtain swags are equally tempting, and Colorcasa also stocks wonderfully warm *trapunti* (quilted bed-covers) in vivid fabrics.

🚩 F5 ☒ Campo San Polo, San Polo 1989–91 ☎ 041 523 6071 ⛴ San Tomà N, 1, 2

MARIANO FORTUNY

Fortuny was born in Catalonia, Spain in 1871, the son of a painter and fabric collector. He moved to Venice when he was 18, soon gaining renown in fields ranging from physics and chemistry to architecture and theater design. Today, he is best remembered for his fabrics, and in particular for the pleated dresses he created that were so fine they could be rolled up and threaded through a wedding ring.

DANIELA GHEZZO

danielaghezzo.it

This is a very serious bespoke shoe store for people who truly love shoes and appreciate exquisite and traditional craftsmanship. The expertise is traditional but the designs are fresh and imaginative, shoes and sandals made using beautiful leathers of every type.

➕ H6 ✉ Calle dei Fuseri, San Marco 4365 ☎ 041 522 2115 🚤 Rialto 1, 2

EBRÛ

albertovalese-ebru.it

The owner of this shop, Alberto Valese, was at the cutting edge of the 1970s revival in Venetian marbled paper. His shop takes its name from the traditional Turkish marbling technique used to create many of his products.

➕ F6 ✉ Campo Santo Stefano, San Marco 3471 ☎ 041 523 8830 🚤 Giglio 1

EMILIO CECCATO

emilioceccato.com

If there is one souvenir, over and above glass, that greets you at every turn in Venice, it is the fake and mass-produced gondolier's straw hat. This unique little shop sells the genuine article, together with the rest of the gondolier's garb—hats, tunics and trousers.

➕ H5 ✉ Sottoportego di Rialto, San Polo 1617 ☎ 041 522 2700 🚤 Rialto N, 1, 2

F.G.B.

fgb-muranoglass.com

This long-established store, housed in a charming casinetto in the center of the campo, sells all the traditional Venetian souvenirs at some of the best prices in town. There are glass pieces in clear and milk colors, beads and earrings,

ANTIQUES

Bric-a-brac and antiques bargains are rare in a city that is acutely aware of its past and the value of its *objets d'art*. Still, Venice provides an almost unlimited choice of beautiful things to buy. There are shops around Campo Santo Stefano in San Marco, or head for Venice's most famous dealer, Pietro Scarpa (➕ F7 ✉ Calle Contarini, Dorsoduro 1023a ☎ 041 523 9700).

paper products and much more besides, including gifts for children.

➕ G7 ✉ Campo Santa Maria del Giglio, San Marco 2514 ☎ 041 523 6556 🚤 Giglio 1

FONDACO DEI TEDESCHI

dfs.com

Built by German merchants in the Middle Ages as their Venice headquarters, the iconic Fondaco dei Tedeschi overlooks the Grand Canal next to the Rialto Bridge. It was used for many years as the post office and has now been stunningly restored as a high-end shopping center, featuring luxury clothing and beauty brands, as well food and wine. There are superb views from the top terrace and an elegant bar-restaurant.

➕ H5 ✉ Calle del Fontego dei Tedeschi, San Marco 32 ☎ 041 314 2000 🚤 Rialto 1, 2

GALLERIA LIVIO DE MARCHI

liviodemarchi.com

You will probably see examples of Livio de Marchi's work as you walk around Venice: everyday objects such as socks, umbrellas or hanging shirts lovingly and precisely carved of wood. You may not actually need a wooden tie,

Beautiful Venetian handmade paper

but the works are unique and make fun souvenirs.

🔲 F6 ⊠ Calle del Dose, Corte da Ponte, San Marco 2742/a ☎ 041 528 5694
🔳 Sant'Angelo or San Samuele N, 1, 2

GIANNI BASSO

Going into Gianni Basso's *stampatore* will take you back in time. The huge old printing presses are still in action, making business cards for people all over the world. Gianni has resisted change—he doesn't have a website and takes orders by mail only. He also sells beautiful lithographs of Venice then and now.

🔲 J2 ⊠ Calle del Fumo, Cannaregio 5306 ☎ 041 523 4681 🔳 Fondamente Nove N, 1, 4.1, 4.2, 5.1, 5.2, 13

GILBERTO PENZO

veniceboats.com

What more appropriate gift or souvenir to take home from Venice than a gondola? This shop sells beautiful handmade wooden models of the boats, as well as gondola prints, posters and simple models (perfect for children) either as kits or ready-made and painted.

🔲 F5 ⊠ Calle II Saoneri, San Polo 2681 ☎ 041 524 6139 🔳 San Tomà N, 1, 2

GOLDONI

By common consent the best general bookshop in Venice, Goldoni has a wide range of literature on the city, along with a limited selection of English and other foreign-language titles.

🔲 H6 ⊠ Calle dei Fabbri, San Marco 4742 ☎ 041 522 2384 🔳 Vallaresso N, 1, 2

JESURUM

jesurum.it

Jesurum has been making exquisite household linens since the 19th century. There are sheets, towels, tableware, pillows, cushions and throws, all made of the finest linen and cotton and edged with lace or trimmed with beautiful bindings. Designs are both classic and contemporary.

🔲 G6 ⊠ Calle Veste, San Marco 2025 ☎ 041 523 8969 🔳 Giglio 1 or Sant'Angelo 2

SHOPPING FOR GOOD

Few visitors realize that Venice has two state prisons, one for men and one for women. Since 2009, the men's prison workshops have been producing stylish shopping bags, wallets, purses and tote bags, which are sold in a concept store near the Frari (Malefatte Venezie 🔲 F5 ⊠ Fondamenta dei Frari, San Polo 2559a ☎ 041 524 3125). The shop is run by Rio Terà dei Pensieri co-op, which also organizes the fabulous weekly organic farmer's market on the Giudecca, selling produce grown by inmates of the women's prison (Orto delle Meraviglie 🔲 F9 ⊠ Calle Convertite, Giudecca 712).

This small but atmospheric market (🕐 Mon–Sat 8–1), just outside the north gates of the Via Garibaldi (gardens), sells fish, *salumeria* (cooked and cured meats), fruit and vegetables. If you are visiting the Museo Storico Navale or the Biennale, it is worth taking a look and enjoying a relatively tourist-free experience; if you're buying, prices are among the city's lowest.

LEGATORIA POLLIERO

This tiny, old-fashioned book-binder's studio alongside Santa Maria Gloriosa dei Frari offers a lovely selection of leather-bound and marbled paper stationery, together with handmade gifts, prints on textiles and beautiful individual sheets of paper.

➕ F5　✉ Campo dei Frari, San Polo 2995
☎ 041 528 5130　🚊 San Tomà N, 1, 2

LIBRERIA ACQUA ALTA

This quirky shop, close to St Mark's Square, is a one-off, with its cluttered interior dominated by a full-size gondola serving as a book display stand, and its walls stacked high with new and second-hand books, magazines and maps. The multilingual owner is a real enthusiast; the accent of the stock is on Venice, and you'll also find photos, posters and gifts. It's a must for lovers of books.

➕ J5　✉ Calle Longa Santa Maria Formosa, Castello 5176　☎ 041 296 0841　🚊 San Zaccaria 1, 2

LIBRERIA TOLETTA

latoletta.com

The Libreria is an excellent bookshop with a huge range of coffee-table books on Venice, guidebooks, Italian classics, art and cookery books—and they're all offered with a good discount.

➕ E7　✉ Calle Toletta, Dorsoduro 1214
☎ 041 523 2034　🚊 Ca' Rezzonico

MARINA & SUSANNA SENT

marinaesusannasent.com

For a more contemporary take on Murano glass, this shop has funky vases, plates and jewelry that won't break the bank. It sells lovely glass pebbles, too.

➕ F7　✉ Campo San Vio, Dorsoduro 669
☎ 041 520 8136　🚊 Accademia N, 1, 2

MURANERO

muranero.venezia.it

Niang Moulaye from Senegal became fascinated with Venetian glass-making when he came to Italy as a student. He learned the craft of bead-making and today makes beautiful, solid necklaces and bracelets in vibrant shades and designs inspired by Africa.

➕ L6　✉ Salizada del Pignater, Castello 3545　☎ 347 649 7947, 338 450 3099
🚊 Arsenale 1, 4.1, 4.2

NICOLA TENDERINI

fontegoart.it

Nicola is a gifted watercolorist who sells her paintings as they are and also uses them as designs for tex-tiles, scarves, bags, bookmarks, calendars and cards. The shop is an excellent source for easily car-ried small gifts for friends back home, with a good range of prices.

➕ E7　✉ Shop: Ramo Toletta, Dorsoduro 1183/b; studio: Campo Bella Vienna, San Polo 216　☎ Shop: 041 523 8691; studio: 041 522 6532　🚊 Shop: Accademia/Ca' Rezzonico 1, 2; studio: Rialto Mercato 1

SHOP

O STORE

obag.it

O Store was launched in 2009 with the aim of creating watches and bags that were totally customizable and individual to every wearer. Mix and match from a range of 120 watch faces and 36 strap colors—the watches snap in and out of the strap. Bags can be custom made, or you can choose from the ever-changing selection.

⊞ H4 ✉ San Giovanni Crisostomo, Cannaregio 5692 ☎ 041 522 6442 🚤 Rialto 1, 2

LA PADOVANA

This leather store pulls in locals and visitors, all attracted by the classic, middle-range shoes, boots and accessories for men and women. They may not be at fashion's cutting edge but are well made, and you'll often find seasonal offers.

⊞ J6 ✉ SS Filippo e Giacomo, Castello 4272 ☎ 041 522 4106 🚤 San Zaccaria 1, 2

PANTAGRUELICA

Pantagruelica is one of the finest food shops in Venice, offering the best produce from all over Italy, including a great selection of local wines. The emphasis is on quality, with plenty of organic produce. The enthusiastic owner is always happy to spend time talking to customers about the food producers he patronizes.

⊞ E6 ✉ Campo San Barnaba, Dorsoduro 2844 ☎ 347 511 9802 🚤 Ca' Rezzonico 1

PAPEROOWL

paperoowl.com

Both workshop and store, this pretty little outlet specializes in paper—all the usual products are here. What makes it special is the jewelry made of paper. Also look for the charming 3D cards "Venice in a Box."

⊞ F4 ✉ Calle Longa, San Polo 2155a ☎ 041 476 1974 🚤 Riva de Biasio N, 1, 2

IL PAPIRO

This fine little shop, with branches around the world, sells marbled paper as well as handsome desk objects, cards, notebooks, diaries and other pretty stationery. There are two other outlets in the city.

⊞ G6 ✉ Calle del Piovan, San Marco 2764 ☎ 041 522 3055 🚤 Giglio 1

PIED À TERRE

piedaterre-venice.com

This tiny shop, behind the market stalls at the foot of the Rialto bridge, has the best selection in Venice of *friulani*, lovely velvet slippers that come in myriad jewel-bright colors, with non-slip soles made of recycled bicycle tyres—comfortable, hard-wearing and quintessentially Venetian.

⊞ H4 ✉ Ruga d'Orefici, 60 Rialto/San Polo 60 ☎ 041 528 5513 🚤 Rialto Mercato 1

THE RIALTO

As a district, the Rialto is almost as old as the city itself, the earliest settlers having been attracted to its high banks, or *rivo alto*, which formed a dry and easily defended redoubt amid the marsh and mud of the lagoon. While San Marco developed into the city's political heart, the Rivoaltus became its commercial hub, where all manner of staple and exotic goods were traded in the "Bazaar of Europe."

TESSITURA BEVILACQUA

luigi-bevilacqua.com

Velvets, damasks and brocades of unrivaled sumptuousness are woven on traditional machines by this old Venetian family business, founded in 1875. These fabrics are world famous and exported everywhere. Buy by the meter or perhaps snap up a luxurious cushion or brocaded purse.

➕ F3 ✉ Campiello della Camare, Santa Croce 1320 ☎ 041 721 566 🚤 Riva di Biasio 1, 5.1, 5.2

TRAGICOMICA

tragicomica.it

Superb handmade masks, created by an artist trained at Venice's Accademia delle Belle Arti, echo the 18th-century heyday of *Carnevale*. Look for Harlequins, Columbines, the plague doctor and mythological masks.

➕ F5 ✉ Calle dei Nomboli, San Polo 2800 ☎ 041 721 102 🚤 San Tomà N, 1, 2

VENETIAN DREAMS

Marisa Convento is an *impiraressa*, Venetian for a woman who makes glass jewelry beads. And what beads these are—beads like pearls, beads like corals, beads of multi-colored and multi-textured glass. If you are lucky, you may find her working in the tiny shop/atelier.

➕ G6 ✉ Calle della Mandola, San Marco 3805a ☎ 041 523 0292 🚤 Sant'Angelo 1

VENETIA STUDIUM

venetiastudium.com

Inspired by Fortuny, this beautiful store offers sumptuous lamps, textiles and accessories, in fabrics ranging from richly colored figured velvet and damask to silk and satin, while the lamps are based on the original Fortuny designs. It's pricey, but a clutch bag or scarf make the perfect Venetian souvenir.

➕ G7 ✉ Calle del Bastion, Dorsoduro 180/a ☎ 041 523 6935 🚤 Salute 1 or Accademia 1, 2

ZAZÙ

Here, fabrics are natural and the cut is beautiful, on items such as draped tops, voluminous trousers tapering at the ankle and bias-cut skirts in softest jersey, all style trademarks. Strong colors are used alongside grey and black, or tones of sand and off-white.

➕ F5 ✉ Calle dei Saoneri, San Polo 2750 ☎ 041 715 426 🚤 San Tomà 1, 2

Entertainment

Once you've done with sightseeing for the day, you'll find lots of other great things to do with your time in this chapter, even if all you want to do is relax with a drink. In this section, establishments are listed alphabetically.

Introduction

If Venice is beautiful beyond words by day, at night it's possibly lovelier still. With the daytrippers gone, most streets and alleys away from the main squares are eerily quiet, perfect for a late stroll in the velvet summer darkness.

Night-time Enchantment

Most visitors to Venice have only a few nights to enjoy the city's night-time atmosphere, and there's no better way to do so than taking a walk off the beaten track. Venice is one of the safest cities anywhere, so you should have no worries about exploring its dark streets. Wherever you go, you'll find yourself ambling through an atmospheric world of medieval corners and narrow streets that open up to views enhanced by the combination of darkness and artificial light. Moonlight glistens on the water and the only sounds are distant, echoing footsteps and the slap of water on stone–magical indeed. Round it off with a nightcap or copy the locals and buy a *gelato* (ice cream) to enjoy as you go.

What's On

This is all very well for a few nights, but the evening may come when you're looking for entertainment. It has to be said that the choice is limited, and you won't find many clubs, pubs or thumping music: Venice goes to bed

DARK WATERS

Few things are more enchanting than a trip down the Canal Grande under a starlit sky. Indeed, it is almost worth organizing your arrival in the city for nightfall, so that you can approach your hotel by *vaporetto* or water taxi under the cover of darkness: It may be the most memorable part of your trip. And if you are going to lavish a small fortune on a gondola ride, make sure it is at night. Better still, take it in the silent, dark-dappled canals away from the main waterways.

Clockwise from top: Live music entertains patrons of Caffè Florian; the Canal Grande; a couple standing near fairy lights on a canal bridge; viewing artists' work on

remarkably early. Scattered throughout the city, though, are late-night bars, many with live music at least two or three times a week, and a handful of clubs. Follow the students to Campo Santa Margherita, where there's plenty of late music, or head to northern Cannaregio, where the Fondamenta della Misericordia has a string of late-opening bars. For something a bit more elegant, you could hit the tables at the casino, housed right on the Canal Grande in a stunning palazzo.

The Cultural Scene

Many visitors take advantage of Venice's cultural life, which is surprisingly vibrant for what is, in essence, a small provincial city. There are concerts of Venetian music virtually every evening, many featuring performers dressed in 18th-century costumes playing Vivaldi against the backdrop of some beautiful *salone* in a sumptuous palazzo. The opera season at the wonderful Fenice runs from September until June, and city theaters stage frequent concerts as well as occasional dance performances.

To see what's on while you're there, pick up a copy of the day-by-day listings magazine, *Un Ospite di Venezia*, published monthly and available from tourist information offices and some hotels, or online at unospitedivenezia.it.

VALUE FOR MONEY

If you're watching the budget, you can have a great-value evening by taking a *vaporetto* trip up or down the Canal Grande and alighting at San Marco or the Accademia. From San Marco you can stroll along the Riva degli Schiavoni, with its fabulous evening views, while the Accademia stop gives access to the Zattere, a sheltered quayside with views to the Giudecca, benches and Nico (▷ 149), one of the best *gelaterie*. Other options include taking a picnic to the Lido, window-shopping in the upmarket streets of San Marco, or great people-watching.

Piazza San Marco; Basilica di San Marco illuminated in the dark; a night-time view from Ponte dell'Accademia

Directory

SAN MARCO
Live Entertainment
Venezia the Show
Music Clubs and Bars
Bacaro Jazz
B Bar Lounge
Torino@Notte
Vino Vino
Theater, Opera and Classical Music
Musica in Palazzo
Scuola Grande di San Teodoro
Teatrino Grassi
Teatro La Fenice

CANNAREGIO
Live Entertainment
Casinò Municipale di Venezia
Music Clubs and Bars
Algiubagio
Paradiso Perduto
Zenevia
Theater, Opera and Classical Music
Teatro Malibran
Cinema
Cinema Multisala Giorgione Movie D'Essai

CASTELLO
Music Clubs and Bars
Giorgione

Theater, Opera and Classical Music
Fondazione Querini Stampalia

SAN POLO AND SANTA CROCE
Cinema
Arena di Campo San Polo
Music Clubs and Bars
Caffè dei Frari
Do Mori
Theater, Opera and Classical Music
Chiesa di San Giacometto
Palazzetto Bru Zane
Santa Maria Gloriosa dei Frari
Scuola Grande di San Giovanni Evangelista

DORSODURO
Music Clubs and Bars
Cantina del Vino già Schiavi
Orange
Piccolo Mondo
Round Midnight
Venice Jazz Club
Theater, Opera and Classical Music
Santa Maria della Salute

Entertainment A–Z

ALGIUBAGIO
algiubagio.net
Right by the *vaporetto* landing stage, this busy, modern and welcoming bar is a good place for a warming or reviving drink and snack while waiting for, or after disembarking from, a boat. Or drop by during a stroll around the farther reaches of Cannaregio.

🞖 J3 ✉ Fondamenta Nuove, Cannaregio 5039 ☎ 041 523 6084 🕓 Wed–Mon 7am–midnight 🚤 Fondamente Nove 4.1, 4.2, 5.1, 5.2, 12, 13, 21, 22

ARENA DI CAMPO SAN POLO
For two weeks every August this large *campo* plays host to a pop-up outdoor cinema, with seating for audiences of up to 200 people.

The backdrop of flickering hues across crumbling Venetian buildings adds to the drama. Films range from mainstream blockbusters to festival hits, and are usually dubbed into Italian.

🔢 F5 ✉ Campo San Polo, San Polo 📞 For details check invenicetoday.com 🚤 San Silvestro 1, San Tomà N, 1, 2

BACARO JAZZ

bacarojazz.it

The fabulous Cuban *barista* (barman) here does his utmost to make you feel welcome, and mixes a mean mojito. Expect plenty of jazz and *gondolieri* enjoying themselves. There is good food, too.

🔢 H5 ✉ Salizzada del Fontego dei Tedeschi, San Marco 5546 📞 041 528 5249 ⏰ Daily 12pm–2am 🚤 Rialto N , 1, 2

B BAR LOUNGE

bauervenezia.com

Upscale and quietly luxurious, this supremely comfortable bar is located in the Bauer, one of Venice's ritziest hotels, and is often referred to simply as "the Bauers." Drinks and service are everything you could want, there's often jazz and live blues, particularly in winter, and more than a bit of celebrity spotting.

🔢 H7 ✉ Salita San Moise, San Marco 1459 📞 041 520 7022 ⏰ Daily 6pm–midnight 🚤 San Marco Vallaresso 1, 2

CAFFÈ DEI FRARI

This is a great place for an aperitif, especially if you want to dine nearby. Many Venetians start their night with the house spritz or a glass of Prosecco.

🔢 F5 ✉ Fondamenta dei Frari, San Polo 2564 📞 041 476 7305 ⏰ Daily 8am–9pm. Closed 15 days in Aug 🚤 San Tomà N, 1, 2

CANTINA DEL VINO GIÀ SCHIAVI

cantinaschiavi.com

Here is an old-fashioned wine bar that really looks the part, set almost opposite San Trovaso and one of Venice's few remaining gondola workshops.

🔢 E7 ✉ Fondamenta Nani-Meravegie, Dorsoduro 992 📞 041 523 0034 ⏰ Mon–Sat 8.30–8.30 🚤 Accademia or Zattere N, 1, 2, 6, 8

CASINÒ MUNICIPALE DI VENEZIA

casinovenezia.it

Venice's popular Casinò Municipale (Municipal Casino), one of only a handful in Italy, is housed in the impressive Palazzo Vendramin-Calergi. Dress code is smart—a jacket and tie for men. Guests must be over 18 and bring ID.

🔢 F3 ✉ Palazzo Vendramin-Calergi, Calle Larga Vendramin, off Rio Terrà della Maddalena, Cannaregio 2040 📞 041 529 7111 ⏰ Daily 2.45pm–2.30am 🚤 San Marcuola N, 1, 2 💶 Expensive

EVENING PASTIMES

Venice does not have the riotous nightlife to match other major Italian cities. For many Venetians, an evening out consists of a meal or drink with friends in a fine restaurant, rounded off with a stroll to a bar for a coffee or ice cream. One of the best places to join them is on an attractive square such as Campo San Polo (🔢 F5). *Scuole* and churches are also popular for classical music concerts.

CHIESA DI SAN GIACOMETTO

This intimate church of San Giacomo di Rialto, affectionately known as San Giacometto, near the Rialto markets, is considered to be the oldest in Venice. It hosts concerts by the Ensemble Antonio Vivaldi and other guest orchestras.

H4 ⊠ Campo di San Giacometto, San Polo 30125 ☎ 041 426 6559 🚊 Rialto, San Silvestro 1

CINEMA MULTISALA GIORGIONE MOVIE D'ESSAI

A good selection of art-house films is shown at this two-screen Cannaregio cinema. Hollywood films are often dubbed into Italian.

H4 ⊠ Rio Terrà dei Franceschi, Cannaregio 4612 ☎ 041 522 6298 🚊 Ca' d'Oro N, 1

DO MORI

The most atmospheric of Venice's old-time *bacari* (▷ panel below) has been in business since 1462, and is always bustling with people from the nearby Rialto markets. It serves good snacks, and stocks 350 wines. All guests must stand.

G4 ⊠ Calle do Mori, San Giovanni, San Polo 429 ☎ 041 522 5401 ⏱ Mon–Sat 8.30–8.30 🚊 Rialto N, 1, 2

FONDAZIONE QUERINI STAMPALIA

querinistampalia.it

This cultural institution organizes a diverse selection of artistic events, with regular Friday and Saturday classical concerts held in the opulent surroundings of a 15th-century palazzo *salone*.

J5 ⊠ Campiello Querini Stampalia, Castello 5252 ☎ 041 271 1411 🚊 Rialto N, 1, 2 and all services to San Zaccaria

GIORGIONE

ristorantegiorgione.it

Venetians flock to this trattoria and pizzeria for the quality food, Friulian wines and Venetian folk music. The owner, Lucio Bisutto, is one of the art's leading exponents and frequently performs his all-singing and a little dancing "fisherman's tales."

M7 ⊠ Via Giuseppe Garibaldi, Castello 1533 ☎ 041 522 8727 ⏱ Thu–Tue 11.30–3.30, 6–10.30 🚊 Giardini N, 1, 4.1, 4.2, 5.1, 5.2

MUSICA IN PALAZZO

musicapalazzo.com

Watch grand opera on a small scale in the evocative surroundings of the 18th-century Palazzo Barbarigo Minotto. Performances of some ever-popular operas, such as *La Traviata* and *The Barber of Seville*, take place in the state rooms of the palazzo, with performers singing their roles among the members of the audience.

G7 ⊠ Palazzo Barbarigo Minotto, Fondamenta Barbarigo, San Marco 2504 ☎ 39 340 971 7272 ⏱ Peformances daily 8.30pm 🚊 Giglio 1

WINE BARS

Old-fashioned wine bars, or *bacari,* are a Venetian way of life. One of the city's more civilized habits is the custom of breaking up the day with an *ombra* ("shadow"), a small glass of wine that takes its name from the idea of escaping the heat of the sun for a restorative tipple. A small snack, or *cichetto,* usually accompanies the drink. An *enoteca* is a more refined bar, with a greater choice of wines and a range of reasonably priced meals.

ORANGE

orangebar.it

Orange spritz is the signature drink in this orange-themed bar, restaurant and champagne lounge. There's an upstairs terrace where you can watch life on the Campo, but most of the chic clientele are busy watching each other.

🔲 E6 ✉ Campo Santa Margherita, Dorsoduro 3054/a ☎ 041 523 4740 🕐 Daily 8am–2am 🚢 Ca' Rezzonico 1

PALAZZETTO BRU ZANE

bru-zane.com

The Palazzetto Bru Zane opened in 2008 as the venue for around 100 concerts annually, all themed to aspects of the 19th-century French Romantic movement, either a composer, a specific instrument or a musical theme. This is a good contrast to Venice's staple musical diet of 18th-century Italian offerings. Some concerts are given in the Scuola Grande di San Rocco.

🔲 E4 ✉ Calle dell'Ogio, San Polo 2368 ☎ 041 521 1005 🕐 Phone or check website for times and schedules 🚢 San Tomà, Piazzale Roma

PARADISO PERDUTO

ilparadisoperduto.wordpress.com

The atmosphere at this renowned nightspot makes up for the fairly average food that is served here. The inexpensive wine and eclectic music attract a diverse, alternative crowd, and its legendary all-night theme parties have sometimes made it unpopular with the locals over the years.

🔲 G2 ✉ Fondamenta della Misericordia, Cannaregio 2540 ☎ 041 720 581 🕐 Thu–Mon 11–3, 6–2 🚢 Madonna dell'Orto 4.1, 4.2, 5.1, 5.2

CARNEVALE

Venice's famous carnival takes its name from the Latin *carnem levare*, or *carne vale*—the "farewell to meat." It probably began in the city's 15th-century private clubs. Resurrected in 1979 (by a group of non-Venetians), it emulates the great pre-Lenten festivals of the 18th century: Thousands of tourists dressing in masks and extravagant costumes indulge in a series of events. Today, the carnival lasts 10 days (up to the beginning of Lent).

PICCOLO MONDO

piccolomondo.biz

This may not be the most fashionable, and it is probably the smallest, but Piccolo Mondo is one of Venice's few nightclubs.

🔲 F7 ✉ Calle Contarini Corfù, Dorsoduro 1056/a ☎ 041 520 0371 🕐 Tue–Sun 11pm–4am 🚢 Accademia N, 1, 2

ROUND MIDNIGHT

This intimate club attracts all sorts for the mainstream music. It features occasional live acts, which are popular with students.

🔲 E6 ✉ Calle dei Pugli, off Fondamenta dello Squero, Dorsoduro 3102 ☎ 041 523 2056 🕐 Mon, Wed–Sat 10pm–4am 🚢 Ca' Rezzonico 1

SANTA MARIA GLORIOSA DEI FRARI

chorusvenezia.org
basilicadeifrari.it

There are sacred music concerts here in spring and autumn, sometimes featuring orchestral ensembles, other times organ recitals. The church makes a great setting for music.

🔲 E5 ✉ Campo dei Frari, San Polo ☎ 041 272 8618 🕐 Phone for latest details 🚢 San Tomà N, 1, 2

Bright lights in Riva degli Schiavoni

SANTA MARIA DELLA SALUTE

This is the venue for a variety of classical organ music. As well as performances by the lead organist of the basilica, guest performers also appear as part of Sunday Mass at 11am every week.

➕ G7 ✉ Campo della Salute, Dorsoduro 1 ☎ 041 522 5558 ⏰ Phone for latest details 🚢 Salute 1

SCUOLA GRANDE DI SAN GIOVANNI EVANGELISTA

scuolasangiovanni.it

The stunning main hall of this important *scuola grande* is the backdrop for spring and autumn performances of some of Italy's best-loved operas. Book online or buy your tickets at the door.

➕ E5 ✉ Campiello della Scuola, San Polo 2454 ☎ 041 718 234 ⏰ Feb–May, Sep–Oct; telephone or check website for times and schedules 🚢 San Tomà, Piazzale Roma

SCUOLA GRANDE DI SAN TEODORO

Plunge yourself back into the 18th century at a performance by this musical group, based in a stunning palazzo near the Rialto. The performers wear appropriate costume for their turn-of-the-18th-century repertoire, mixed with later opera favorites.

➕ H5 ✉ Campo San Salvador, San Marco 481 ☎ 041 521 0294 🚢 Rialto 1, 2

TEATRO LA FENICE

teatrolafenice.it

This famous opera house (▷ 75) hosts a full schedule of operas and other concerts, and you can also join a daytime tour to see the fabulous interior.

➕ G6 ✉ Campo San Fantin, San Marco 1965 ☎ 041 786 672; information 041 2424; for tickets fenice.artacom.it/biglietteria 🚢 Giglio 1

TEATRINO GRASSI

palazzograssi.it

It's worth visiting the superb architectural space of the Teatrino Grassi even if you don't attend one of the screenings, concerts or lectures regularly held here. The 225-seat auditorium occupies what was the garden behind the Palazzo Grassi and was designed by the minimalist architect Tadao Ando as the third stage (2013) of the Palazzo Grassi project.

WHAT'S ON

Details of films, concerts and exhibitions in Venice are listed in the *Spettacoli* section of daily editions of local newspapers such as *Il Gazzettino* and *La Nuova Venezia*. *Un Ospite di Venezia*, a free Italian/English magazine available from hotels and tourist offices, also contains detailed listings (published weekly in peak season, monthly during the off season). Tourist offices always have plenty of posters and leaflets on current events. Also keep an eye out for posters on the streets.

F6 Campo San Samuele, San Marco 3231 041 241 308 San Samuele 2, Sant'Angelo 1

TEATRO MALIBRAN

teatrolafenice.it

A theater has stood on this site since 1677, and was Venice's most elite performance venue throughout the 18th century. It became the Teatro Malibran in 1835 in honor of soprano Maria Malibran, who donated her fee to its refurbishment. Today the theater stages well-known operas such as *La Traviata* and more modern works, as well as occasional Shakespeare plays in Italian, classical concerts and first-class ballet productions.

H4 Calle dei Milion, Cannaregio 041 965 1975 Rialto N, 1, 2

TORINO@NOTTE

Live jazz, beer, spritz and toasted sandwiches make up the staple diet of the fun-loving crowd here. The action spills out onto the *campo* during the summer and during Carnival.

H5 Campo San Luca, San Marco 459 041 522 3914 Tue–Sat 7.30pm–1am Rialto N, 1, 2

VENEZIA THE SHOW

teatrosangallo.net

If you want an entertaining look at the history of Venice, the nightly shows here combine live action with state-of-the-art video, music and sound presentations to evoke the history of the city and the atmosphere of Carnival—touristy, but good fun.

H6 Campo San Gallo, San Marco 1097 041 241 2002 Performances daily 7pm San Marco Vallaresso, San Marco Giardinetti 1, 2 Expensive

VENICE JAZZ CLUB

venicejazzclub.com

The VJC quartet, made up of piano, drums, double bass and guitar, is a passionate group of experienced jazz artists who play a varied repertoire of old favorites and new tunes; they have frequent guest artists too.

E6 Ponte dei Pugni, Dorsoduro 3102 340 150 4985 Mon–Wed, Fri–Sat 9pm–11pm Ca' Rezzonico 1

VINO VINO

vinovinowinebar.com

Rather more showy and smarter than some of Venice's humbler bars, this two-roomed spot close to the opera house has more than 100 different wines to accompany its snacks and meals.

G6 Ponte delle Veste, Calle delle Veste, San Marco 2007a 041 241 7688 Daily 11.30–11.30 Giglio 1

ZENEVIA

This bar is popular for its intimate nooks inside and its seating outside on Campo Santa Maria Formosa. There is occasional live music.

J5 Campo Santa Maria Formosa, Cannaregio 5548 041 520 6266 Wed–Mon 9pm–2am Zattere, Rialto

WHERE TO GO

Nightlife in Venice is decidedly low key. Late-night possibilities are really limited to bars and live-music cafés, where you can hear jazz, blues or reggae, with the occasional Latino or rock session. A main party area is Fondamenta della Misericordia in Cannaregio, where a string of waterfront bars and tiny clubs transforms the whole quayside into one long nightspot.

ENTERTAINMENT

Eat

There are places to eat across the city to suit all tastes and budgets. In this section, establishments are listed alphabetically.

Introduction

Venetian cooking is as individual as the city, with the accent on fish and seafood, but there is also meat, game and vegetables from the lagoon islands, and rice, polenta and pasta. Avoid places offering a *menù turistico*, and expect prices to be high.

When to Eat

Breakfast is usually served between 8 and 10. Locals often pop into a bar on their way to work for a cappuccino and a *briosc* (pastry). Venetian restaurants popular with locals operate two timescales—one for them and one for visitors. Working Venetians eat lunch between 12 and 1 and dinner between 8 and 9. Restaurants aimed mainly at tourists start lunch at 12.30 and dinner at 7, though some serve throughout the day.

Where to Eat

Like many Italian cities, there is a confusing array of eating places. A *ristorante* tends to be expensive, whereas the trattoria is less formal, less expensive, and often family-run. Such places may not have a printed menu, and the waiter will reel off a list of what's on offer; many speak enough English to help you choose. *Osterie* were basic, and some still are, but the term is often synonymous with good food and rustic elegance. *Pizzerie* in Venice tend to open all day; ovens are electric so Venetian pizzas aren't as good as in Rome or Naples.

WHAT TO EAT

A full Venetian meal is gargantuan—antipasti, a *primo* (first course) of soup, rice or pasta, a *secondo* (main course) of fish with vegetable *contorni* (side dishes), then *formaggi* (cheese) and *dolce* (dessert). Do as the locals do and pick and mix. Few Venetians eat either cheese or dessert in restaurants, preferring to head for a *pasticceria* or choose a *gelato* (ice cream) if they want something sweet to round off a meal.

From top: Caffè Florian; fritelle (small doughnuts) are a popular snack; outdoor tables at Caffè Florian; Osteria la Zucca

EAT

Directory

SAN MARCO
Cafés and Bars
Caffè Florian
Teamo
Fine Dining
Harry's Bar
Fish and Seafood
Acquapazza
Al Conte Pescaor
Ice Cream
Paolin
Trattorie and Osterie
Osteria al Bacareto
Osteria I Rusteghi

CANNAREGIO
Trattorie and Osterie
Osteria l'Orto dei Mori
Venetian
Anice Stellato
Trattoria Cea
Vini Da Gigio

CASTELLO
Fish and Seafood
Al Mascaron
Corte Sconta
Trattorie and Osterie
Alla Rivetta
Da Remigio
Osteria alle Testiere
Osteria Oliva Nera

SAN POLO AND SANTA CROCE
Cafés and Bars
Bottega del Caffè Dersut
Ciak
Fine Dining
Poste Vecie
Fish and Seafood
Da Ignazio
Italian
Antica Birraria la Corte

Pizzerie
Ae Oche San Giacomo
Muro Venezia Frari
Il Refolo
Trattoria and Osterie
Osteria la Zucca
Trattoria San Tomà
Venetian
Alla Madonna
Antiche Carampane
Bancogiro
Ribó

DORSODURO
Cafés and Bars
Improntacafe
Fine Dining
Antica Locanda Montin
Ice Cream
GROM
Nico
Pizzerie
Casin dei Nobili
Venetian
La Bitta
Dona Onesta
Taverna San Trovaso

EAT

Eating A–Z

ACQUAPAZZA €€–€€€

veniceacquapazza.com
The accent is mainly on fish: Starters may include prawns and rocket with balsamic dressing and a seafood platter; follow with the catch of the day or a fish risotto.
🔲 G6 ⊠ Campo Sant'Angelo, San Marco 3808 ☎ 041 277 0688 🕐 Apr–Oct daily lunch and dinner; Nov–Mar closed Mon 🚇 Sant'Angelo

AE OCHE SAN GIACOMO €–€€

aeochesangiacomo.it
Usually heaving with students, this lively pizzeria serves thin, crisp pizzas with a huge range of toppings and a few pasta dishes.
🔲 F4 ⊠ Calle del Tintor, San Giacomo, Santa Croce 1552/A ☎ 041 524 1161 🕐 Daily lunch, dinner 🚇 Riva di Biasio 1

AL CONTE PESCAOR €€

alcontepescaor.it
This wonderful tiny fish restaurant caters mainly to Venetians, despite its proximity to Piazza San Marco.

🔲 J6–H6 ⊠ Piscina San Zulian, San Marco 544 ☎ 041 522 1483 🕐 Mon–Sat lunch and dinner. Closed Jan 🚇 San Marco Vallaresso, San Marco Giardinetti N, 1, 2

ALLA MADONNA €€

ristoranteallamadonna.com
One of the most authentic and one of the oldest restaurants in the city, Alla Madonna has the look of a Venetian restaurant of 30 years ago. It is popular for business meetings and family celebrations. The food is rigorously Venetian.
🔲 H5 ⊠ Calle della Madonna, San Polo 594 ☎ 041 522 3824 🕐 Thu–Tue lunch and dinner. Closed 2 weeks in Aug 🚇 Rialto N, 1, 2

ALLA RIVETTA €€

This inexpensive but good small trattoria close to Piazza San Marco makes a pleasant alternative to some of the more expensive places. It is often very busy.
🔲 J6 ⊠ Ponte San Provolo, near Campo SS Filippo e Giacomo, Castello 4625 ☎ 041 528 7302 🕐 Tue–Sun lunch and dinner. Closed Aug 🚇 All services to San Zaccaria

AL MASCARON €€

osteriamascaron.it
This nice old bar-trattoria has a brisk, informal atmosphere, a beamed ceiling and black-and-white photos on the walls. Fish

Caffè Florian

Antica Locanda Montin

and seafood is served, and it is so popular (reservations essential) that the owners have opened Alla Mascareta for wine and snacks at No. 5183.

➕ J5 ✉ Calle Lunga Santa Maria Formosa, Castello 5225 ☎ 041 522 5995 🕐 Mon–Sat lunch and dinner. Closed mid-Dec to mid-Jan 🚤 Rialto N, 1, 2

ANICE STELLATO €€

osterianicestellato.com

The "Star Anise" combines its role as a down-to-earth *bacaro* (wine bar) with that of a rustically elegant trattoria serving traditional Venetian food. You may find the bar area packed with locals but, once you have found a table, you can enjoy a delicious meal, its dishes entirely dependent on the season and what's available in the market. For a light lunch, choose saucers of *cichetti* (snacks) accompanied by an *ombra*, a glass of local white wine.

➕ F2 ✉ Fondamenta della Sensa, Cannaregio 3272 ☎ 041 720 744 🕐 Tue–Sat lunch and dinner, Mon dinner 🚤 Sant'Alvise 4.1, 4.2, 5.1, 5.2

ANTICA BIRRARIA LA CORTE €€

birrarialacorte.it

This converted warehouse is one of a new breed of Venetian restaurants. The seating spills out into evocative Campo San Polo, making it perfect for sunny days and balmy evenings. The inside is contemporary, with clean lines and chrome. The food nods to all the Venetian and Italian classics—it's good quality. You can snack or go the whole hog here.

➕ F5 ✉ Campo San Polo, San Polo 2168 ☎ 041 275 0570 🕐 Daily 10am–midnight; kitchen 12–3, 6–10.30 🚤 San Silvestro 1

ANTICA LOCANDA MONTIN €€

locandamontin.com

This venerable restaurant, not far from the Gallerie dell'Accademia, has been famous for decades and is popular with the rich and famous, although today it does depend somewhat on its former reputation. The quality of food is now once again touching previous heights; eat in the painting-lined dining room or on the shaded outside terrace to the rear.

🔲 E7 ✉ Fondamenta di Borgo, Dorsoduro 1147 ☎ 041 522 7151 🕐 Tue dinner, Thu–Mon lunch and dinner 🚤 Zattere or Ca' Rezzonico N, 1, 2, 5.1, 5.2, 6, 8

ANTICHE CARAMPANE €€€

veneziaristoranti.it

One of the association of Buona Accoglienza restaurants, whose members aim to promote traditional Venetian cooking and hospitality, this off-the-beaten-track restaurant specializes in beautifully cooked, elegantly served seafood and fish. The style is a modern take on tradition, seen at its best in dishes such as *spaghetti alla granseola* (spaghetti with spider crab), *cassopipa* (pasta with a spicy fish sauce) or *branzino in salsa di peperoni* (sea bass in sweet pepper sauce). The wine list is long, desserts elegant and imaginative, but booking is essential.

🔲 G4 ✉ Ponte delle Tette, San Polo 1911 ☎ 041 524 0165 🕐 Tue–Sat lunch and dinner 🚤 San Stae/Rialto Mercato

BANCOGIRO €€

osteriabancogiro.it

Housed in one of the 16th-century buildings around the markets, the Bancogiro is a welcoming restaurant that doubles as a bar serving *cichetti*. The menu relies on local, seasonal ingredients, prepared

with a modern twist by chef Jacopo Zamboni. The brick-vaulted interior is understated and elegant, and the outside tables are set right beside the Canal Grande.

🔲 H4 ✉ San Giacometto, San Polo 1220 ☎ 41 523 2061 🕐 Tue–Sun 9am–midnight 🚤 Rialto Mercato 1

LA BITTA €€

There's no fish on the menu here, but the meat is farm-sourced, and it's one of the best places to sample *fegato alla veneziana*, the classic Venetian dish of liver and onions served with creamy polenta.

🔲 E6 ✉ Calle Lunga San Barnaba, Dorsoduro 2753/a ☎ 041 523 0531 🕐 Mon–Sat dinner 🚤 Ca' Rezzonico 1

BOTTEGA DEL CAFFÈ DERSUT €

Huge windows allow a glimpse into the interior of this popular café, where you can stand at the bar or relax on one of the deep sofas while you enjoy a specialty coffee—different flavors, offered with a host of toppings, many laced with cream—or get a vitamin fix in the form of a blended veggie juice or mixed-fruit smoothie made to order. They also serve pastries, tarts and cakes.

🔲 E5 ✉ Campo dei Frari, San Polo 3014 ☎ 041 524 5322 🕐 Daily breakfast, snacks all day 🚤 San Tomà

EAT

CAFFÈ FLORIAN €–€€€

caffeflorian.com

The oldest, prettiest and most expensive of Venice's famous cafés has been serving customers since 1720. It was once favored by Lord Byron and the German poet Goethe. Prices are high, but treat yourself for the experience and the chance to admire the interior.

⊞ H6 ⊠ Piazza San Marco, San Marco 56–59 ☎ 041 520 5641 ⌚ Daily 9am–midnight; breakfast, light lunch, snacks all day ⛴ San Marco Vallaresso, San Marco Giardinetti N, 1, 2

CASIN DEI NOBILI €–€€

There's the attraction of a buzzing student atmosphere and eating outside in the pretty garden in summer at this bustling pizzeria/restaurant. The menu features all the solid Venetian classics, but, if you're watching the pennies, pizza is the best bet.

⊞ E6 ⊠ Sottoportego del Casin dei Nobili, Dorsoduro 2765 ☎ 041 241 1841 ⌚ Tue–Sun 12–10.30 ⛴ Ca' Rezzonico 1

CIAK €

A pleasant, relaxed bar, used by everyone from gondoliers to society ladies to adjourn to after visiting Santa Maria Gloriosa dei Frari and the Scuola Grande di San Rocco. They do good lunchtime snacks and sandwiches.

⊞ F5 ⊠ Campiello San Tomà, San Polo 2807 ☎ 041 528 5150 ⌚ Daily breakfast, snacks all day ⛴ San Tomà N, 1, 2

CORTE SCONTA €€

veneziaristoranti.it

Many Venetians and visitors alike rate the popular Corte Sconta as their preferred restaurant, despite its slightly peripheral location. Fairly

small and always busy, its cooking and seafood are rarely less than excellent. There is no menu, so try to follow waiting staff's recommendations. The garden has tables in summer.

⊞ L6 ⊠ Calle del Pestrin, Castello 3886 ☎ 041 522 7024 ⌚ Tue–Sat lunch and dinner ⛴ Arsenale 1, 4.1, 4.2

DA IGNAZIO €€

veneziaristoranti.it

This fairly small, predominantly fish restaurant lies just east of Campo San Tomà, and has the atmosphere of a restaurant from the 1950s. There is a lovely vine-shaded garden for alfresco dining in summer.

⊞ F5 ⊠ Calle Saoneri, San Polo 2749 ☎ 041 523 4852 ⌚ Sun–Fri lunch and dinner. Closed 3 weeks in Jul and Aug ⛴ San Tomà N, 1, 2

DA REMIGIO €€

Small local trattorias are a dying breed in Venice, so this authentic restaurant, despite a redecoration that has removed some old-fashioned touches, is a find. It has just 40 seats, so you will need to reserve or arrive early to share a table. The food is reliable and

EAT

Cherry sorbet and deep-fried custard

homey, the pasta and fish are good, and although the wine list is short it is perfectly adequate.

🔲 K6 ✉ Salizzada dei Greci, Castello 3416 ☎ 041 523 0089 🕐 Wed–Sun lunch and dinner, Mon dinner. 🚢 Arsenale 1, 4.1, 4.2 or all services to San Zaccaria

DONA ONESTA €€

trattoriadonaonesta.eatbu.com

The "Honest Woman" lives up to its name with fine classic food—try the risotto—at budget prices. It is becoming increasingly well known, however, so try to reserve a table in its single small dining room overlooking a little canal midway between San Pantalon and San Tomà.

🔲 E5 ✉ Calle della Dona Onesta, Dorsoduro 3922 ☎ 041 710 586 🕐 Daily 12–10 🚢 San Tomà N, 1, 2

GROM €

A nationwide chain, GROM has made a big impact with its ices. Flavors change monthly, and nothing is on offer unless it's in season. There is another branch at Strada Nuova (Ca' d'Oro), in Cannaregio.

🔲 E6 ✉ San Barnaba, Dorsoduro 2761 ☎ 041 241 3531 🕐 Sun–Fri 12–10, Sat 12–11 🚢 Ca' Rezzonico

HARRY'S BAR €€€

cipriani.com

This legendary establishment is best known for its celebrity status (▷ 146 panel). The restaurant upstairs serves reliable fare, while snacks can be ordered at the downstairs bar. This is *the* place for cocktails—the famous Bellini was invented here.

🔲 H7 ✉ Calle Vallaresso, San Marco 1323 ☎ 041 528 5777 🕐 Lunch and dinner. The bar is open every day but may close during Carnival 🚢 San Marco Vallaresso, San Marco Giardinetti, N, 1, 2

IMPRONTACAFE €–€€

improntacafevenice.com

Dorsoduro is university territory and this lively, modern bar and restaurant, with its late opening hours, pulls in crowds of students and young visitors. You can have breakfast, a light lunch, full dinner or just a drink, and find a buzzy atmosphere. There's a good range of wines by the glass.

MORE OPTIONS

A fixed-price tourist menu *(menù turistico)* usually includes a basic pasta, main course, fruit and half-bottles of wine and water. Food quality is often indifferent—you will probably find many of the same dishes listed on the menu in a budget trattoria as in most expensive restaurants. The difference is primarily in ambience and detail. The *prezzo fisso* (fixed price) menu usually excludes cover, service and beverages. Check what is included in the price.

EAT

E5 ✉ Calle dei Preti Crosera, Dorsoduro 3815 ☎ 041 275 0386 🕒 Mon–Sat breakfast, lunch, dinner and snacks 🚌 San Tomà 1, 2

MURO VENEZIA FRARI €–€€

murovenezia.com

Dark wood and minimalist design bring a feeling of space to this all-day bar and eatery, where the menu offers a good range of pizzas as well as standard Italian and Venetian dishes.

F5 ✉ Rio Tera dei Frari, San Polo 2604b/c ☎ 041 524 5310 🕒 Fri–Wed lunch and dinner 🚌 San Tomà

NICO €

gelaterianico.com

Plan a walk in the Dorsoduro district so that you pass this small waterfront bar renowned for its ice cream, in particular a praline concoction known as *gianduiotto*.

E8 ✉ Zattere ai Gesuati, Dorsoduro 922 ☎ 041 522 5293 🕒 Fri–Wed breakfast, lunch and snacks 🚌 Zattere N, 2, 5.1, 5.2, 6, 8

OSTERIA AL BACARETO €€

bacareto.it

This well-placed traditional trattoria is in a quiet corner of the city just a few moments' walk west of the church of Santo Stefano. You can have a full meal, snack or a plate of antipasti with a glass of wine.

F6 ✉ Calle Crosera, San Marco 3447 ☎ 041 528 9336 🕒 Mon–Fri lunch and dinner, Sat lunch 🚌 Sant'Angelo or San Samuele N, 1, 2

OSTERIA ALLE TESTIERE €€

osterialletestiere.it

It can be hard to get a reservation at this small osteria. The food is inexpensive given the quality that cooking a limited menu for small numbers allows the owner to achieve. The focus is on local dishes, imaginatively prepared and crammed full of zinging tastes.

J5 ✉ Calle del Mondo Novo, Castello 5801 ☎ 041 522 7220 🕒 Mon–Sat, seatings at 7 and 9.15pm 🚌 Rialto N, 1, 2

OSTERIA I RUSTEGHI €

airusteghi.com

Venice is famous for its panini and *tramezzini* (filled rolls and sandwiches) and this tiny place offers well over 30 varieties, which you can enjoy with a beer or glass of wine from the long list.

H5 ✉ Campiello del Tintor, San Marco 5513 ☎ 338 760 6034 🕒 Mon–Sat lunch 🚌 Rialto 1, 2

OSTERIA L'ORTO DEI MORI €€

osteriaortodeimori.com

There aren't many restaurants in northern Cannaregio, and this is a hit with both locals and tourists. The interior looks as if it's been there for years, with warm paneling and shining glass, but the

---

DRINKS

Venice's tap water is perfectly safe to drink, though Venetians prefer mineral water *(acqua minerale)*—either sparkling *(gassata)* or still *(liscia, naturale* or *non gassata)*. Bottles come in one litre *(un litro* or *una bottiglia)* or half-litre *(mezzo litro* or *mezza bottiglia)* sizes. Bottled fruit juice is *un succo di frutta*, available in pear *(pera)*, apricot *(albicocca)*, peach *(pesca)* and other flavors. Fresh juice is *una spremuta*, while milkshake is *un frullato*, or *un frappé* if made with ice cream. Lemon soda is a popular and refreshing bitter lemon drink. Ice is *ghiaccio*, and a slice of lemon is *uno spicchio di limone*.

menu is decidedly 21st century, with Venetian specialities given a modern twist. Everything is well-sourced, short and seasonal; they refuse to use frozen ingredients.
➕ G2 ✉ Campo dei Mori, Cannaregio 3386 ☎ 041 524 3677 ⏰ Wed–Mon lunch and dinner 🚤 Orto 4.1, 4.2, 5.1, 5.2

OSTERIA LA ZUCCA €€
lazucca.it

The imaginative and ever-changing food in this pleasantly located osteria, especially the vegetable side dishes and main courses, is innovative, at least by Venice's normally conservative standards.
➕ F4 ✉ Calle del Tintor (or Tentor), Santa Croce 1762 ☎ 041 524 1570 ⏰ Mon–Sat lunch and dinner 🚤 Riva di Biasio 1, 5.1, 5.2

OSTERIA OLIVA NERA €€€
olivanera.com

This is one of a new breed challenging the old school of Venetian restaurateurs. Its mostly fish and seafood menu shows Venetian cooking can be given a contemporary edge. All fish is fresh from the market. Oliva Nera II, in the same street at No. 3447 (closed Thursday), offers a more meat-based menu while retaining the same principles of fresh home cooking.
➕ K6 ✉ Salizzada dei Greci, Castello 3417–18 ☎ 041 522 2170 ⏰ Thu–Tue 12–2.30, 7–10 🚤 Services to San Zaccaria

PAOLIN €–€€
The best café in one of Venice's nicest squares has lots of outside tables and very good ice cream. It's definitely worth a stop.
➕ F6 ✉ Campo Santo Stefano (Campo Francesco Morosini), San Marco 2962 ☎ 041 522 5576 ⏰ Daily breakfast, snacks and ice cream. Closed Dec–Jan 🚤 Accademia N, 1, 2

POSTE VECIE €€€
postevecie.com

Ingredients could hardly be fresher at this appealing fish restaurant, reputedly founded in 1500, along-side the Pescheria fish market. Cooking is refined, but can be variable, and there's a good wine list.
➕ H4 ✉ Campo della Pescaria, San Polo 1608 ☎ 041 721 822 ⏰ Wed–Mon lunch and dinner. Closed 4 weeks in Jul and Aug 🚤 Rialto N, 1, 2

IL REFOLO €
In a quiet corner near a church, this is popular with locals for good pizzas and a limited selection of pastas and main courses.
➕ F4 ✉ Campo San Giacomo dell'Orio, Santa Croce 1459 ☎ 041 524 0016 ⏰ Tue dinner, Wed–Sun lunch and dinner. Closed Nov–Mar 🚤 Riva di Biasio or San Stae 1

RIBÓ €€€
This is a refreshingly bright and modern restaurant, serving light and modern Venetian cuisine, and a little off the usual tourist trail.

EAT

ETIQUETTE

The procedure when standing up in a bar is to pay for what you want at the cash desk *(la cassa)* and take your receipt *(lo scontrino)* to the bar, where you repeat your order (a tip slapped down on the bar works wonders with the service). Do not then take your drink and sit at an outside table, as you will pay a premium to sit down and order through a waiter. However, if sitting, a single purchase allows you to relax almost indefinitely.

Expect reasonable (though not low) prices, superb fresh pasta and fresh fish, and a romantic interior patio garden.

🚏 D5 ✉ Fondamenta Minotto, Santa Croce 158 ☎ 041 524 2486 🕐 Thu–Tue lunch and dinner. Closed 2 weeks in Aug 🚤 San Basilio N, 2, 6, 8

TAVERNA SAN TROVASO €

tavernasantrovaso.it

With its attractive neutral decor, lively atmosphere and reliable cooking, the San Trovaso is popular with Venetians so reserve ahead (especially for Sunday lunch). The desserts are especially tasty.

🚏 E7 ✉ Calle Contarini Corfù, Dorsoduro 1016 ☎ 041 520 3703 🕐 Daily lunch and dinner 🚤 Accademia N, 1, 2

TEAMO €

teamowinebar.com

This sleek, relaxing, modern wine bar makes a good change of pace from the traditional Venetian snack bar. There's a wide range of *cichetti* at lunch, including both hot and cold fish- or meat-based dishes, or you could try a platter of mixed smoked meats and cheeses.

🚏 G6 ✉ Rio Terà della Mandola, San Marco 3795 ☎ 041 528 3787 🕐 Daily lunch and snacks 🚤 Giglio 1

TRATTORIA CEA €–€€

trattoriacea.com

This truly Venetian eating house has been satisfying the neighborhood for years and you could be the only foreigner here. There's a good-value set menu at lunch, or go à la carte and choose from the short menu of mainly fish dishes. If you want to sample *baccalà mantecato* (creamed, dried salt cod), this is the place to try it.

🚏 J4 ✉ Campiello Widmann, Cannaregio 5422/a ☎ 041 523 7540 🕐 Mon–Fri lunch and dinner, Sat lunch 🚤 Fondamente Nove 4.1, 4.2, 5.1, 5.2

TRATTORIA SAN TOMÀ €–€€

trattoriasantoma.com

The pizzas and trattoria food served here are good, but this restaurant's best attraction is its location, only one minute south of Santa Maria Gloriosa dei Frari and the Scuola Grande di San Rocco.

🚏 F5 ✉ Campo San Tomà, San Polo 2864 ☎ 041 523 8819 🕐 Summer daily lunch and dinner; winter Wed–Mon lunch and dinner 🚤 San Tomà N, 1, 2

VINI DA GIGIO €€

veneziaristoranti.it

Pretty, relaxed and romantic, this restaurant is on a peaceful canal and has two simple beamed rooms and old cabinets. Venetian cooking includes fish and meat dishes, and a short, well-chosen wine list.

🚏 G3 ✉ Fondamenta della Chiesa-San Felice, Cannaregio 3628a ☎ 041 528 5140 🕐 Wed–Sun lunch and dinner. Closed Jan and 3 weeks in Aug 🚤 Ca' d'Oro N, 1

EAT

Sleep

Venice has a great range of places to stay, with options to suit all tastes and budgets. In this section, establishments are listed alphabetically.

SLEEP

Introduction

Compared with its population, Venice has more tourist accommodation than any other Italian city. This ranges from 5-star luxury through cutting-edge boutique hotels to low-key, family-run traditional establishments and numerous bed and breakfasts. Despite this, for much of the year Venice remains a seller's market, reflected in the high price of all its accommodations.

What to Expect

Venetian hotels are classified by the Italian state system into five categories from 1 to 5 stars (basic to luxury), which reflect facilities rather than room size or decor. Room prices may alter according to the season and all prices must be displayed in the foyer and on the back of bedroom doors; check to see if breakfast is included in this. There are often considerable savings on rack rates by booking online or as part of a package. It's acceptable to ask to see the room; the hotel may have cheaper options than the first room you're shown.

Where to Stay

San Marco has many places to stay and is the heart of the city, but is also very noisy and constantly crowded by day. To the east, Castello is both quieter and cheaper, while to the west Cannaregio has enormous choice, with many budget options near the railway station. Across the Canal Grande, San Polo and Santa Croce have family-run, traditional hotels, particularly around the Rialto, while Dorsoduro, a largely residential area, makes a peaceful choice.

FEELING THE HEAT

Venice is very hot in the summer, so a courtyard or garden is a bonus, as are rooms away from the street. Bear in mind that noise bounces off water and narrow streets, especially if they are major thoroughfares.

From the top: Hotel Palazzo Stern; Accademia-Villa Maravege; detail of a stained-glass window at the Danieli hotel; a red-carpeted staircase in the Danieli

SLEEP

154

Directory

SAN MARCO
Budget
Fiorita
Mid-Range
Al Piave
Flora

SAN POLO AND SANTA CROCE
Budget
Ai Due Fanali
Ai Tolentini
Iris
La Villeggiatura
Mid-Range
Oltre il Giardino

CANNAREGIO
Mid-Range
Ca' Dogaressa

CASTELLO
Budget
Canada
Doni
Locanda Silva
Mid-Range
Ai Due Principi
Locanda la Corte
Luxury
Danieli

DORSODURO
Budget
Ca' Foscari
Mid-Range
Accademia-Villa Maravege
Hotel American Dinesen
La Calcina
Pensione Seguso
San Sebastiano Garden
Luxury
Ca' Maria Adele
Centurion Palace
Palazzo Stern

Sleeping A–Z

PRICES	
Prices are approximate and based on a double room for one night.	
€€€€	€501–€800
€€€	€351–€500
€€	€176–€350
€	€90–€175

ACCADEMIA-VILLA MARAVEGE €€

pensioneaccademia.it

This 17th-century *palazzo*, west of the Accademia, once housed the Russian Embassy. Its charming rooms are grand and furnished with antiques, although some are small. The lovely garden has a good view of the Canal Grande.

⊞ E7 ⊠ Fondamenta Bollani, Dorsoduro 1058 ☎ 041 521 0188 ⛴ Accademia N, 1, 2

AI DUE FANALI €

aiduefanali.com

Set on a tranquil *campo* just back from the Canal Grande, yet only 10 minutes from the station and Piazzale Roma, many of this hotel's comfortable rooms have canal views. Rooms are traditionally furnished, and some are rather small, though they have terracotta and marble bathrooms. There's a roof terrace for summer breakfasts.

⊞ E3 ⊠ Campo San Simeon Grande, Santa Croce 946 ☎ 041 718 490 ⛴ Riva di Biasio 1, 5.1,5.2

AI DUE PRINCIPI €€

hotelaidueprincipi.com

The more expensive rooms of this boutique hotel have views over Campo San Zaccaria or the canal in front; they are lofty and spacious, while the bathrooms are state of the art. The public areas are chic and comfortable.

⊞ K6 ⊠ Fondamenta dell'Osmarin, Castello 4971 ☎ 041 241 3979 ⛴ Services to San Zaccaria

AI TOLENTINI €

albergoaitolentini.it

If you're looking for a simple, excellent-value hotel, the Tolentini, a few minutes' walk from Piazzale Roma, is a good find. The immaculate rooms are on the small side, but some have canal views and the beds are comfortable. Breakfast is not served, but there are bars close by.

⊞ D5 ⊠ Calle Amai, Santa Croce 197 ☎ 041 275 9140 ⛴ Piazzale Roma

AL PIAVE €€

hotelalpiave.com

This 27-room hotel is located near Campo Santa Maria Formosa and offers good value for Venice. Rooms are traditional with good, modern bathrooms, and it's family-run, ensuring a high level of customer service.

⊞ J5 ⊠ Ruga Giuffa, San Marco 4838–50 ☎ 041 528 5174 ⛴ San Marco Vallaresso, San Marco Giardinetti, Rialto N, 1, 2

CA' DOGARESSA €€

cadogaressa.com

Ca' Dogaressa is a good bet in Cannaregio, where so many hotels are on the busy stretch from the station. The hotel, in an 18th-century palazzo on the Canale di Cannaregio, has charming waterside views. The decor is traditionally Venetian, with beamed ceilings, brocade and Murano glass chandeliers. The owners go out of their way to help guests enjoy Venice.

⊞ D2 ⊠ Fondamenta di Cannaregio, 1018 Cannaregio ☎ 041 275 9441 ⛴ Tre Archi 4.1, 4.2, 5.1, 5.2

A hotel near the Ponte Scalzi

Many hotels now occupy restored palazzi

CA' FOSCARI €

locandacafoscari.com

This relaxed and well-appointed 1-star hotel has 11 rooms (five with private bathroom) and is hidden away in an alley.

➕ E6 ✉ Calle della Frescada, Dorsoduro 3888/b ☎ 041 710 401 🚤 San Tomà or Ca' Rezzonico N, 1, 2

CA' MARIA ADELE €€€

camariaadele.it

Right next to the Salute and a minute's walk from the *vaporetto*, this luxurious little hotel provides the ultimate in refined and romantic living. Choose between one of the themed suites, where the decor ranges from cozy fireside to oriental, or relax in the comfort of a more conventional room. Breakfast is served in a charming room dominated by an over-the-top Murano glass chandelier.

➕ G7 ✉ Rio Terrà dei Catecumeni, 111 Dorsoduro ☎ 041 520 3078 🚤 Salute

LA CALCINA €€

lacalcina.com

Overlooking the Giudecca canal in elegant Dorsoduro, this long-established hotel has classically comfortable rooms, good facilities and a lovely waterfront terrace.

➕ F8 ✉ Fondamenta Zattere ai Gesuati and Fondamenta Vernier, Dorsoduro 780 ☎ 041 520 6466 🚤 Zattere 2, 5.1, 5.2, 6, 8

CANADA €

canadavenice.com

This immaculate 25-room hotel has several singles. The best room (a double) has its own roof terrace. Reserve in advance.

➕ J5 ✉ Campo San Lio, Castello 5659 ☎ 041 522 9912 🚤 Rialto N, 1, 2

CENTURION PALACE €€€–€€€€

sinahotels.com

Set where the Canal Grande opens out into the Bacino, the Centurion fuses a sensitive reconstruction of a historic building with 21st-century taste and style. Rooms are superbly equipped and comfortable in a modern fashion, while the restaurant, lounges and bar overlook the Canal Grande.

➕ G7 ✉ Campo San Gregorio, Dorsoduro 173 ☎ 041 34281 🚤 Salute

DANIELI €€€–€€€€

danielihotelvenice.com

A hotel since 1822, the Danieli is the choice of visiting royalty and VIPs. It ranks as the finest of Venice's luxury hotels—but stay in the old wing of the Gothic palazzo rather than the newer annexe.

➕ J6 ✉ Riva degli Schiavoni-Calle delle Rasse, Castello 4196 ☎ 041 522 6480 🚤 San Zaccaria 1, 2

DONI €

albergodoni.it

The Doni is an intimate hotel between the Basilica and San Zaccaria where some of the simple rooms (four with bathroom) overlook the Riva del Vin or the garden.

⊞ K6 ⊠ Calle del Vin, off Salizzada San Provolo, Castello 4656 ☎ 041 522 4267 🚊 All services to San Zaccaria

FIORITA €
locandafiorita.com
This pretty, popular hotel is in a quaint square (used for breakfast in summer) just north of Santo Stefano. The rooms (with private bath) have beamed ceilings.
⊞ F6 Ⓜ Campiello Novo, San Marco 3457/a ☎ 041 523 4754 🚊 Accademia or Sant'Angelo N, 1, 2, 4

FLORA €€
hotelflora.it
This good-sized hotel has a well-deserved reputation, thanks to its pleasant garden. Some rooms are rather small. It is just off the south side of Calle Larga (Viale) XXII Marzo, west of Piazza San Marco.
⊞ G7 ⊠ Calle Bergamaschi, San Marco 2283a ☎ 041 520 5844 🚊 Giglio 1

HOTEL AMERICAN DINESEN €€
hotelamerican.com
The American is two minutes' walk from the Accademia, on a small canal, and offers traditional decor combined with streamlined facilities. There's a lovely terrace for evening drinks.
⊞ F7 ⊠ Fondamenta Bragadin, Rio di San Vio, Dorsoduro 628 ☎ 041 520 4733 🚊 Accademia N, 1, 2

IRIS €
hotelirisvenice.com
The Iris is in a quiet area of San Polo near the Frari church. The guest rooms are light and simply furnished; not all have private bathrooms, but each has a TV, hairdryer and telephone.
⊞ E5 ⊠ Fondamenta dei Forner, Calle del Cristo, San Polo 2910/a ☎ 041 522 2882 🚊 San Tomà

LOCANDA LA CORTE €€
locandalacorte.it
This delightful hotel was home to a Venetian noble family in the 16th century, and its rooms maintain a historic and luxurious look but with modern amenities. The inner courtyard, where breakfast is taken, is a special treat.
⊞ J5 ⊠ Calle Bressana, Castello 6317 ☎ 041 241 1300 🚊 Fondamente Nove 5.2

LOCANDA SILVA €
locandasilva.it
The Silva is in a lively *calle* between Santa Maria Formosa and San Marco. The public areas, including the breakfast room, have modern furniture and fittings, while bedrooms are light, modern and functional. Some have pleasant canal views but the lowest-priced ones share a bathroom.
⊞ J5 ⊠ Fondamenta di Remedio, Castello 4423 ☎ 041 522 7643 🚊 Services to San Zaccaria

---

RESERVATIONS
It is now almost essential to reserve a room in Venice for July and August, and wise to do so during the rest of the peak season, which officially runs from 15 March to 15 November and from 21 December to 6 January, and now in effect includes the period of *Carnevale* in February. Many hotels do not recognize a low season, however, and lower-category hotels where you might have been able to negotiate lower off-season rates often close in winter. Check out the internet for the best deals.

SLEEP

Since 1822, when the Danieli (▷ 157) opened, Venice hasn't been short of top hotels. Plenty of new kids on the block have arrived, catering for a well-heeled, but younger and trendier crowd. Type "boutique hotels Venice" into a search engine for a wide choice. For peace and quiet, consider the luxury of the Cipriani (cipriani.grandluxuryhotels.com), set in gardens on Giudecca island) or San Clemente Palace (kempinski.com), with a lagoon island to itself, pool, spa and tennis courts. It is connected to the city by private launch.

OLTRE IL GIARDINO €€–€€€

oltreilgiardino-venezia.com

This beautiful and quiet hotel, tucked away near the Frari and surrounded by its garden, feels in many ways like a private house. Rooms are understated, furnished with a beguiling mix of antique and new; the *salotto* (sitting room) has inviting sofas, an honesty drinks tray and books to read.

➕ F5 ✉ Fondamente Contarini, San Polo 2542 ☎ 041 795 452 🚤 San Tomà 1, 2

PALAZZO STERN €€–€€€

palazzostern.com

For a room with a view, check into the Stern, one of Venice's prettiest Gothic Canal Grande palazzi. The breakfast terrace is set on the water; inside, an overhaul restored the interior to its Gothic-Moorish appearance, the work of the 19th-century owner. Rooms are traditionally furnished in Venetian style, and there's a rooftop jacuzzi with great city views.

➕ E6 ✉ Calle del Traghetto, Dorsoduro 2792/a ☎ 041 277 0869 🚤 Ca' Rezzonico 1

PENSIONE SEGUSO €–€€

pensionesegusovenice.com

Founded early in the 20th century by a British diplomat, the Seguso combines charming old-fashioned style and service with modern comfort. Rooms are furnished with antiques and retain their traditional *terrazza* floors, some have canal views but not all have bathrooms. There is a restaurant and outside seating area but no WiFi.

➕ F8 ✉ Fondamente Zattere ai Gesuati, Dorsoduro 779 ☎ 041 528 6858 🚤 Zattere 2, 5.1, 5.2

SAN SEBASTIANO GARDEN €€

hotelsansebastianogarden.com

Tucked away on a quiet canal just back from the Giudecca canal, this comfortable hotel is housed in a thoughtfully renovated old palazzo. All is space and calm in the public areas, while the bedrooms are large, traditionally decorated and comfortable. The chief draw, perhaps, is the lovely garden.

➕ D6 ✉ Fondamenta San Sebastiano, Dorsoduro 2542 ☎ 041 523 1233 🚤 San Basilio 2, 6, 8

LA VILLEGGIATURA €–€€

lavilleggiatura.it

It's worth the climb to the third floor to this airy, light-filled bed and breakfast near the Rialto, with its individually styled and spacious rooms. Wooden floors, lamps, textiles and paintings add character; the bathrooms are bright and modern. Breakfasts are ample and served in a beautifully traditional Venetian *salotto*.

➕ G4 ✉ Calle dei Botteri, San Polo 1569 ☎ 041 524 4673 🚤 Rialto Mercato 1

SLEEP

Need to Know

This section takes you through all the practical aspects of your trip to make it run more smoothly and to give you confidence before you go and while you are there.

NEED TO KNOW

Planning Ahead

WHEN TO GO

Avoid July and August, the hottest and busiest months, and plan a visit for April (excluding the busy Easter period), May, June, September or October. Hotels are busy from Easter to October, in February during *Carnevale*, and over Christmas and New Year. Despite the weather, winter can still be a delightful time to see the city.

TEMPERATURE

JAN	FEB	MAR	APR	MAY	JUN	JUL	AUG	SEP	OCT	NOV	DEC
43°F	46°F	59°F	66°F	73°F	74°F	79°F	79°F	70°F	61°F	54°F	45°F
6°C	8°C	12°C	15°C	20°C	23°C	26°C	25°C	21°C	16°C	12°C	7°C

Spring (March to May) has a mixture of sunshine and showers; the chilly easterly wind, the *bora*, can lower temperatures. Fog occurs occasionally.

Summer (June to August) can be unpredictable; clear skies and searing heat one day followed by sultry clouds and thunderstorms the next.

Autumn (September to November) can be glorious, though be prepared for wet days and *acqua alta* (peak tides). November is often wet and foggy with *acqua alta* (high water).

Winter (December to February) *Acqua alta* can occur at any time (including into March); January and early February can be bitterly cold with brilliant sunshine.

WHAT'S ON

February *Carnevale* (Carnival): pageants, masks and costumes.

March *Su e zo per i ponti*: A long road race in which competitors run "up and down the bridges" of Venice (fourth Sunday in Lent).

April *Festa di San Marco*: A gondola race from Sant'Elena to the Punta della Dogana marks the feast day of Venice's patron saint. Men traditionally give women a red rose.

May *La Sensa*: Venice's mayor re-enacts the Marriage to the Sea, in which the doge would cast a ring into the sea to symbolize the "wedding" of the city to the sea (Sunday after Ascension Day).

Vogalonga: Literally the "long row," a 32km (20-mile) race from Piazza San Marco to Burano and back (one Sunday in May).

June *Biennale*: Venice's international art exhibition (Jun–Nov) is in odd-numbered years; the architectural Biennale is in even-numbered years.

July *Festa del Redentore*: Pontoons are laid across the Giudecca canal to the Redentore to celebrate Venice's deliverance from the plague of 1576. People picnic in boats and watch fireworks (third Sunday of the month).

September *Venice Film Festival*: Held on the Lido (late Aug/early Sep).

Regata Storica: Historical costume pageant and procession of boats on the Canal Grande, followed by a race among gondoliers (first Sunday of the month).

November *Festa della Salute*: A pontoon is built on boats across the Canal Grande to the Salute; people cross to light a candle in the church to celebrate the passing of a plague in 1630 (21 Nov).

VENICE ONLINE

veneziaunica.it
Venice's official site for advance booking of reduced-price transportation and sightseeing tickets and passes. Prices fluctuate according to how busy the city will be during your visit, and all services on offer are optional, enabling you to build your own package. Book seven days in advance and collect your tickets on arrival at a Venezia Unica ticket point.

invenicetoday.com
This site, updated daily, is an excellent source of information, though a word or two of Italian is useful. It has accommodations listings, restaurant and bar information, tips for museum and exhibition visits, nightlife, sporting possibilities and current events.

comune.venezia.it
Although aimed as much at local residents as visitors, the city council's site provides good up-to-date information on cultural activities and historic sites in the city. Look here for the latest on erratically opening museums, city services and what's on when. The site is linked to veneziaunica.it.

venezia.net
Italian site with English version. News, general travel information, shopping, a selection of bars, cafés and restaurants, excellent material on museums and main attractions, plus 3D tours of sights.

visitmuve.it
Everything about Venice's museums, including the collections, special exhibitions, opening times, prices, facilities and how to get there. You can also buy your tickets in advance.

Venezia Unica, the app
This free interactive app contains all the information you'll need during your stay and it's updated all the time. There are maps, transportation details, information on culture, shopping, eating, drinking and much more.

USEFUL SITES

actv.avmspa.it
Venice's city transportation system runs this informative site, where you'll find full route details, timetables and fare structures for the *vaporetto* network.

enit.it
The main Italian tourist board website covers the whole country, with plenty of information on Venice.

trenitalia.com
The official site of the Italian State Railways with excellent train information and an easy-to-use search facility—good for forward planning.

fodors.com
A travel-planning site where you can research prices and weather, book tickets, cars and rooms, and ask fellow travelers questions; links to other sites.

INTERNET ACCESS

There are over 200 WiFi hotspots scattered around the historic center of Venice and the islands. Using them will save you money on your roaming charges. You can access the system via the veneziaunica.it website. Packages cost €5 for 24 hours, €15 for 72 hours and €20 for a week. Many hotels also offer free internet access.

Getting There

ENTRY REQUIREMENTS

For the latest passport and visa information, look up the British embassy website at gov.uk/government/world/italy or the United States embassy it.usembassy.gov. EU citizens can obtain health care with the production of the EHIC card. However, insurance to cover illness and theft is strongly advised.

ARRIVING BY CAR

Cars must be left at one of the multistory car parks at the Tronchetto. From here you can catch boat No. 2 to the rest of the city or use the People Mover, a monorail that connects the parking with Piazzale Roma in a couple of minutes, stopping en route at the cruise ship terminal. From Piazzale Roma you can walk or catch boats N, 1, 2, 3, 4.1, 4.2, 5.1, 5.2 or 6. Parking rates start at about €32 a day (veniceparking.it). There are no free car parks and no other parking places; cars parked elsewhere will be towed away and, in summer, long lines on the causeway approaching the city are common. Consider leaving your car in Mestre and then taking the train.

AIRPORTS

There are direct flights to Venice from all over the world. Venice has two main airports, Marco Polo and Canova in Treviso.

Canova Airport
30km (19 miles)
to city center
Bus 1hr, €12

24km (15 miles)
16km (10 miles)
8km (5 miles)

● Venice

Marco Polo Airport
8km (5 miles)
to city center
Bus 20 minutes, €8

FROM MARCO POLO BY ROAD

Scheduled internal and international flights (plus a few charters) arrive at Venice's Marco Polo Airport, 8km (5 miles) north of the city hub. For flight information, call 041 260 9260 or visit veniceairport.it. Connections from Marco Polo to Piazzale Roma take 20–40 minutes and can be made by taxi, blue ATVO Fly/35 bus (atvo.it; hourly from 5.20 to 8.20am, then every 20 minutes from 8.20 to 11pm; €8 one way, €15 return) or less expensive ACTV No. 5 orange city buses (actv.it; 4.08am–1.10am; €3 one-way). Buy tickets for buses from the automatic ticket machines in the baggage reclaim area, in the arrivals hall or next to the bus stop. Buses leave from the concourse outside the terminal.

FROM MARCO POLO BY WATER

There are two options: a regular boat service, run by Alilaguna, or the more expensive option, the water taxi. To get to the water terminal and boats turn left outside the main terminal building; a covered, moving walkway connects with the boat services into Venice. The cheaper option is run by the Società Alilaguna (alilaguna.com) with an hourly boat service from Marco Polo to the city. It costs €15 and goes to San Marco, the Lido and Zattere. Make sure you buy your ticket before you leave the airport—the office is close to the arrivals hall exit.

ROUTES

Of the three central lines, the Alilaguna Rossa goes via Murano, the Lido, the Arsenale and San Zaccaria to San Marco; and the Linea Alilaguna Blu travels via the Lido, the Arsenale, San Marco, the Zattere and the Hilton on the Giudecca to the Cruise Terminal. Choose the service that takes you closest your hotel; you may find that you will have to connect with an ACTV *vaporetto* for the last stages.

● The Blu (blue) services start at 6.10am; thereafter the boat leaves at 7.10, then hourly at 10 minutes past the hour until 3.15pm.

● The Rossa (red) boats start at 9.15am and run hourly until 15 minutes past midnight. Tickets cost €15 and the journey time is 75–90 minutes; the service runs Apr–Oct.

● The Arancio (orange) line runs to the Fondamenta Nove and Santa Maria del Giglio via the Canal Grande half-hourly from 7.45–7.45, then hourly till midnight throughout the year; tickets cost €15.

WATER TAXIS

Water taxis are run by the Consorzio Motoscafi Venezia, whose desk is to the left of the exit from the baggage reclaim area in the airport arrivals hall (tel 041 240 6712 Mon–Fri, 041 522 2303 Sat–Sun; motoscafivenezia.it, veneziataxi.it). The taxis run to most points in the city (25 minutes), but the prices are high (allow at least €100, including baggage surcharges).

FROM TREVISO

Canova airport (tel 042 231 5111; trevisoairport.it), 30km (19 miles) outside the city, is served by low-cost airlines; an ATVO/Eurobus shuttle (atvo.it; €12 each way) connects with some flights. Buy tickets at the ATVO ticket office or foreign exchange outlet.

Trains to Venice arrive at the Venezia Santa Lucia station, often abbreviated as Venezia SL (☎ 892 021 or 199 892 021; from outside Italy 0039 06 684 75475; trenitalia.it). The station is at the head of the Canal Grande, five minutes' walk from Piazzale Roma; from the quays outside there are frequent *vaporetto* (1, 2 and others) and *motoscafo* (5.2) boat services to the rest of the city. Be sure the boat you board is heading in the right direction. Many through trains stop on the mainland at Mestre station (☎ 041 929 472), confusingly called Venezia Mestre (Venezia M), without continuing to Venice proper. Check whether your train is destined for Santa Lucia; if not, catch one of the frequent connecting services at Mestre for the 15-minute trip across the causeway.

Before you leave home, ask your hotel to send you details of how to reach them. You need to know the nearest *vaporetto* stop, the name of the street as well as the *numero civico* (the number given after the district in the address), and the nearest landmark, such as a *campo*, church or museum.

Getting Around

HANDY HINT

Tourist tickets are available for ACTV boats. A 24-hour ticket costs €20, 48-hour €30, 72-hour €40 and 7-day €60. You can buy tickets online at veneziaunica.it, at the ACTV offices at Piazzale Roma and Tronchetto and also at other important *vaporetto* stops.

VISITORS WITH DISABILITIES

Venice is difficult for visitors with impaired mobility. Streets are narrow, there are numerous bridges and moving on and off boats is almost impossible. Hotels, galleries and other public spaces are often in historic buildings where conservation restrictions limit access. This said, matters are improving, and the Venetian and Italian state tourist offices have lists of suitable hotels and contact details of Italian associations for those with disabilities.

GONDOLAS

Hiring a gondola is enchanting, but expensive (starting at around €80 for 40 minutes). Rates are negotiable, so confirm the cost and duration before departure. Do not be afraid to walk away or haggle if the prices seem too high and there are plenty of gondoliers. If cost is an issue, take the cheap public gondolas, the *traghetti*.

The best way to move around Venice is on foot; this is how the Venetians themselves get from place to place, combining walking with the judicious use of public transportation in the shape of *vaporetti* (water buses) and *traghetti* (cross-Canal Grande ferries).

BOATS

● ACTV runs two basic types of boat: the general-purpose *vaporetto* and the faster *motoscafo*. Both follow set routes and are numbered at the front of the boat. As the same number boat may run in two directions it is vital at the quays—which have separate boarding points for each direction—to make sure you board a boat heading the right way. This is particularly true at the Ferrovia and San Zaccaria—both are busy terminals for several routes.

● The web of boat routes around Venice is not as confusing as it first seems. The basic route is Line 1 along the Canal Grande (Piazzale Roma–Vallaresso–Lido and back). Line 2 also follows the Canal Grande, but has fewer stops. A second 2 boat runs from San Zaccaria to Piazzale Roma by way of the Giudecca. The other boat you may use is the No. 12, which runs to the islands of Murano and Burano from the Fondamente Nove. The No. 9 shuttle connects Burano and Torcello. The ferry information throughout this guide gives the nearest stop as well as the line number.

● Tickets can be bought at most landing stages, on board boats (with a surcharge), and at shops or tobacconists with an ACTV sticker. One-way tickets (€7.50, valid for 75 minutes) are valid along the length of the route so the price is the same for one stop or 10 stops. Tickets must be validated by passing them in front of the I-Mob electronic scanner before boarding; a green light will show. If you have a tourist ticket this must be validated every time you use it. There are spot fines for riding without a ticket.

● Special tickets are available (▷ panel).

● ACTV runs a less frequent service with a

reduced number of stops throughout the night on key Canal Grande routes (indicated by "N" throughout the guide). Exact times are posted on the timetables at every quay. Tickets can be bought on board.

TAXIS

● For rides to and from the mainland there are taxi stands at Piazzale Roma, tel 041 595 2080; Marco Polo Airport, tel 041 541 6363; and Mestre rail station, tel 041 936 222. Otherwise, call Radio Taxi, tel 041 5964.

TRAGHETTI

● As there are only four main bridges across the Canal Grande, Venice's *traghetti* (ferries) provide an invaluable service. Think of them as bridges and it becomes clear they will save both time and unnecessary mileage. They exist primarily for the convenience of locals but, once you are familiar with the system, judicious use of the *traghetti* will help you get quickly from point to point. Using large gondolas, they ply back and forth at seven strategic points. Quays are usually obscure, so look for the little green "Traghetto" signs. Crossings cost around €0.80, which you hand to the ferryman as you board. Venetians usually stand, but nobody minds if you sit unless the boat is crowded. Be careful with small children, and watch your balance when the boat pushes off.

WATER TAXIS

● Venice's water taxis (*motoscafi*), a fast but extremely expensive way to travel (▷ 164–165), are grouped into a co-operative of several firms, Motoscafi Venezia. A one-way transfer from the airport to central Venice costs around €120, with surcharges levied for each piece of baggage, and extra charges on public holidays and for each additional passenger over a maximum of four. The easiest, and cheapest, way to book is pre-booking online at motoscafivenezia.it, or by calling the central booking line on 041 240 6712 Mon–Fri, 041 522 2303 Sat–Sun.

TOURIST INFORMATION

● Main tourist offices
☎ 041 2424
veneziaunica.it
● San Marco ✚ H7
✉ Piazza San Marco 71/f
◎ Daily 9–7
● Train station ✚ D4
✉ Ferrovia ◎ Daily 8–6.30
● Piazzale Roma ✚ D5
✉ Vela office ◎ Daily 10–6

LOST PROPERTY

● City streets ☎ 041 274 8225 or visit Vigili Urbani office in Pizzale Roma
● Buses or boats ☎ 041 272 2179 or 041 2424 ◎ Mon–Sat 8–6/4.30 in winter
● Train or station ☎ 041 785 531
● Report lost passports to the police and your consulate
● Report general losses to Questura, the main police ✉ Fondamenta Santa Chiara, Santa Croce 500 ☎ 041 271 5511

Essential Facts

EMBASSIES AND CONSULATES

● Canada ✉ 3 Piazza Cavour, Milan 20121 ☎ 02 6269 4238
● France ✉ (Honorary Consul), Palazzo Morosini, Calle del Pestina, Castello 6140 ☎ 041 522 4319
● Netherlands ✉ San Vidal, San Marco 2888 ☎ 041 528 3416
● Republic of Ireland ✉ Piazza San Pietro in Gessate 2, Milan 20122 ☎ 02 5518 7569
● Portugal ✉ 26 Via Colonnetta 5, Milan 20122 ☎ 02 545 5553
● Spain ✉ 26 Via Fatebenefratelli, Milan 20121 ☎ 02 632 8831
● UK ✉ Via San Paolo 7, Milan 20121 ☎ 02 723 001
● USA ✉ Via Principe Amedeo 2/10, Milan 20121 ☎ 02 290 351

BREXIT

UK visitors should check the very latest entry requirements as a result of the country's decision to leave the EU. Check if a visa is required along with a valid passport and if reduced-cost medical treatment with the European Health Insurance Card (EHIC) is still available. Visit the website gov.uk/visit-europe-brexit.

ELECTRICITY

● Current is 220 volts AC (50 cycles), but is suitable for 240-volt appliances.
● Plugs are the continental two-round-pin.

EMERGENCY PHONE NUMBERS

● Emergency services (police, fire and ambulance), tel 113
● Police (Carabinieri), tel 112
● Questura (Venice Police Station), tel 041 271 5511
● Fire (Vigili di Fuoco), tel 113 or 115
● Ambulance, tel 041 523 0000 or 118
● Hospital and first aid (Ospedale Civile) at Campo SS Giovani e Paolo, tel 041 529 4111

MONEY

● The euro is the official currency of Italy. Bank notes come in denominations of €5, €10, €20, €50, €100 and €200, and coins in denominations of 1, 2, 5, 10, 20 and 50 cents and €1 and €2.
● Foreign-exchange facilities are available at banks and kiosks throughout the city. Major credit cards are widely accepted in Venice and can be used in ATMs displaying the appropriate sign.

NATIONAL HOLIDAYS

● 1 January: New Year's Day; 6 January: Epiphany; Easter Monday; 25 April: Liberation Day; 1 May: Labor Day; 2 June: Republic Day; 15 August: Assumption; 1 November: All Saints' Day; 8 December: Immaculate Conception; 25 December: Christmas Day; 26 December: Santo Stefano

OPENING HOURS

● Banks: Mon–Fri 8–1.30 (larger branches also 3–4 and restricted Sat opening).
● Churches: Non-fixed hours but generally Mon–Sat 9–12, 3–6, Sun 1–5; except St. Mark's and those in the Chorus Group (▷ 4) scheme.
● Shops: Generally daily 9–1, 4–8 or 9.30/10–7.30/8; most food shops close Wed

afternoons except in summer; other shops close Monday mornings except in summer.

POST OFFICES

● Venice's central post office (posta or ufficio postale) is between Piazza San Marco and the Rialto at Calle delle Acque 5016 San Marco (tel 041 240 4149). There are other offices in each sestiere and one on the Giudecca.
● Stamps (francobolli) are available from post offices and tobacconists (tabacchi) displaying a large "T" sign.
● Mailboxes are red or blue and are marked Poste or Lettere. Blue boxes are for faster and more expensive posta prioritaria services only.

SENSIBLE PRECAUTIONS

● Venice's tourists are a target for theft, but with a few precautions you can stay safe. Report thefts to your hotel and then to the main police station. Report lost passports to the police or your embassy.

TELEPHONES

● Telecom Italia (TI) provides public telephones in bars and on the streets. Mobile telephone reception is excellent throughout the city; TIM and Wind are the main providers. You can buy a local pay-as-you-go SIM card from their offices to keep costs down.
● Public phones accept phone cards (schede telefoniche), available from tobacco shops, TI offices, automatic dispensers or stores displaying a TI sticker.
● The area code for Venice is 041 and must be used when calling from both outside and within Venice.

TOILETS

● Venice has public toilets at the rail station and in larger museums. There are public toilets throughout the city marked with blue and green signs. Most cost €1.50 and some have attendants to give change if needed.
● In bars and cafés ask for il gabinetto or il bagno. Do not confuse signori (men) with signore (women).

● Likely hazards include too much sun, air pollution and biting insects.
● Water is safe to drink unless marked acqua non potabile.
● Pharmacies (una farmacia) are identified by a green cross and have the same opening hours as shops, but open late on some days as displayed on pharmacy doors. Staff can give advice on minor ailments and dispense many medicines over the counter, including some only available by prescription in other countries. Remember to bring any prescriptions that might be required to obtain medicine.
● If you wish to see a doctor (un medico), ask at your hotel. For first aid (pronto soccorso) or hospital treatment, visit the Ospedale Civile 🚹 J4 ⊠ Campo Santi Giovanni e Paolo, Castello ☎ 041 529 4111

● In churches do not wear shorts or miniskirts and cover your arms.
● Do not intrude while church services are in progress.
● Do not eat or drink in churches. Many churches and galleries forbid flash photography, or ban photography altogether.

NEED TO KNOW

Words and Phrases

All Italian words are pronounced as written, with each vowel and consonant sounded; only the h is silent. The letter c is hard (as in English "cat"), except when followed by i or e, when it becomes the soft ch of "cello." Similarly, g is soft (as in the English "giant") when followed by i or e—*giardino, gelati*; otherwise hard (as in "gas")—*gatto*. An h after c or g makes it hard even when followed by i or e (*chiesa*). Words ending in o are almost always masculine in gender (plural: -i); those ending in a are generally feminine (plural: -e). Use the polite second person *(lei)* to speak to strangers and the informal second person *(tu)* to friends or children.

NEED TO KNOW

USEFUL WORDS	
yes	*sì*
no	*no*
please	*per favore*
thank you	*grazie*
you're welcome	*prego*
excuse me!	*scusi*
where	*dove*
here	*qui/qua*
there	*lì/là*
when	*quando*
now	*adesso*
later	*più tardi*
why	*perchè*
who	*chi*
may I/can I	*posso*
good morning	*buon giorno*
good afternoon/ good evening	*buona sera*
good night	*buona notte*
hello/goodbye (informal)	*ciao*
hello (on the telephone)	*pronto*
I'm sorry	*mi dispiace*
left/right	*sinistra/destra*
open/closed	*aperto/chiuso*
good/bad	*buono/cattivo*
big/small	*grande/piccolo*
with/without	*con/senza*
more/less	*più/meno*
hot/cold	*caldo/freddo*
early/late	*presto/ritardo*
today/tomorrow	*oggi/domani*
when?/do you have?	*quando?/avete?*

NUMBERS	
1	*uno, una*
2	*due*
3	*tre*
4	*quattro*
5	*cinque*
6	*sei*
7	*sette*
8	*otto*
9	*nove*
10	*dieci*
20	*venti*
30	*trenta*
40	*quaranta*
50	*cinquanta*
100	*cento*
1,000	*mille*

COLORS	
black	*nero*
brown	*marrone*
pink	*rosa*
red	*rosso*
orange	*arancia*
yellow	*giallo*
green	*verde*
light blue	*celeste*
sky blue	*azzuro*
purple	*viola*
white	*bianco*
grey	*grigio*

EMERGENCIES

help!	aiuto!
stop, thief!	al ladro!
can you help me, please?	può aiutarmi, per favore?
call the police/an ambulance	chiami la polizia/un'ambulanza
I have lost my wallet/passport	ho perso il portafoglio/il passaporto
where is the police station?	dov'è il commissariato?
where is the hospital?	dov'è l'ospedale?
I don't feel well	non mi sento bene
first aid	pronto soccorso

USEFUL PHRASES

How are you? (informal)	Come va?
I'm fine	Sto bene
I do not understand	Non ho capito
Do you speak English?	Parla Inglese?
How much is it?	Quant'è?
Do you have a room?	Avete camere libere?
Can I see the room?	Posso vedere la stanza?
I have a reservation	Ho una prenotazione
How much per night?	Quanto costa una notte?
... with bath/shower	... con vasca/doccia
When is breakfast served?	A che ora è servita la colazione?
Where is the train/bus station?	Dov'è la stazione ferroviaria/degli autobus
Where are we?	Dove siamo?
Do I have to get off here?	Devo scendere qui?
I'm looking for ...	Cerco ...
Where can I buy ...?	Dove posso comprare ...?
A table for ... please	Un tavolo per ... per favore
I'm a vegetarian	Sono vegetariano/a
Is there a house specialty?	C'è una specialità della casa?
The bill, please	Il conto, per favore
We didn't have this	Non abbiamo avuto questo
Where are the toilets?	Dove sono i bagni?

DAYS/MONTHS

Monday	lunedì
Tuesday	martedì
Wednesday	mercoledì
Thursday	giovedì
Friday	venerdì
Saturday	sabato
Sunday	domenica
January	gennaio
February	febbraio
March	marzo
April	aprile
May	maggio
June	giugno
July	luglio
August	agosto
September	settembre
October	ottobre
November	novembre
December	dicembre

TIME AND PLACE

morning	mattina
afternoon	pomeriggio
evening	sera
night	notte
today	oggi
tomorrow	domani
yesterday	ieri
early	presto
late	tardi
later	più tardi
when	quando
where	dove
Where is...?	Dov' è...?
Where are we?	Dove siamo?
here	qui/qua
there	lì/là
near	vicino
far	lontano
on the right	a destra
on the left	a sinistra

Index

We would like to thank the following photographers, companies and picture libraries for their assistance in the preparation of this book:

All images are copyright AA/A Mockford & N Bonetti except:

2(i) LOOK Die Bildagentur der Fotografen GmbH/Alamy; 2(ii) Beren Patterson/Alamy; 2(iii) Nic Cleave Photography/Alamy; 2(iv) Alessandro Villa/Alamy; 2(v) imagebroker/Alamy; 3(ii) Matthew Kawalski/Alamy; 3(iii) Kumar Sriskandan/Alamy; 3(iv) Jim Ritchie/Alamy; 5 LOOK Die Bildagentur der Fotografen GmbH/Alamy; 6/7t CHRISTOPHE SIMON/AFP/Getty Images; 6ct an Dagnall/Alamy; 6cb travelstock44/Alamy; 7ct Travelshots.com/Alamy; 6/7b AA/S McBride; 8/9t Gaertner/Alamy; 8cb Alberto Paredes/Alamy; 8b petforsberg/Alamy; 9b Food Features/Alamy; 10l AA, 10r MBP-one/Alamy; 11l AA; 11r MARKA/Alamy; 12 Beren Patterson/Alamy; 14l Paul Carstairs/Alamy; 14/15l AA/C Sawyer; 16 Peter Howard Smith/Alamy; 18/19 The Art Archive/Alamy; 19r Andrea Matone/Alamy; 20l AA/S McBride; 20/21 AA/R Newton; 21r AA/C Sawyer; 22l, 22/23t, 22/23b, 23br © The Peggy Guggenheim Collection; Venice. Photo: Andrea Sarti/CAST1466; 26/7 agefotostock/Alamy Stock Photo; 27tr lowefoto/Alamy; 27cr James Talalay/Alamy Stock Photo; 28/9 John Kellerman/Alamy; 29 AA/D Miterdiri; 30/1 John Kellerman/Alamy; 31tr Adam Eastland Italy/Alamy; 31br Chuck Pefley/Alamy; 32l The Art Archive/Alamy; 32/33 Hackenberg-Photo-Cologne/Alamy; 33r AA/D Miterdiri; 36/37 AA/S McBride; 38/9t © Palazzo Grazzi, ph:Thomas Mayer; 38cl © Palazzo Grazzi, ph:Andrea Jemolo; 38/9c © Palazzo Grazzi, ph:Andrea Jemolo; 39r Luca Da Ros/SIME/4Corners; 40l Biblio Photography/Alamy; 42/43 Vincent MacNamara/Alamy; 43r Angelo Hornak/Alamy; 44/5 AA/S McBride; 47r Worldwide Picture Library/Alamy; 48tl, 48bl, 48/49 AA/C Sawyer; 49r AA/S McBride; 51r adam eastland/Alamy; 52l John Kellerman/Alamy; 52/53 AA/C Sawyer; 54l AA/R Newton; 54/55 AA/S McBride; 57r Michael Harding/Alamy; 58l AA/D Miterdiri; 59br Lonely Planet Images/Alamy; 60/61 Marka/Alamy; 64 Nic Cleave Photography/Alamy; 66 CuboImages srl/Alamy; 67l John Kellerman/Alamy; 68l Collpicto/Alamy; 68r Stefan Nielsen/Alamy; 69l F1online digitale Bildagentur GmbH/Alamy; 69r The Art Archive/Alamy; 70 Fondazione Musei Civici di Venezia; 71l Chuck Pefley/Alamy; 73l David Tomlinson/Alamy; 74 GoneWiththeWind/Alamy; 75l @teatrolafenice; 75r Chris Howarth/Italy/Alamy; 76 Roy Conchie/Alamy; 77 Giovanni Tagini/Alamy; 78 Marco Dotto/Alamy; 79 Stock Italia/Alamy; 80 Alessandro Villa/Alamy; 82t Dave Pattison/Alamy; 83t Ian Dagnall/Alamy; 83b B&Y Photography/Alamy; 86(i) Chris Selby/Alamy; 86(ii) John Kellerman/Alamy; 86(iii) Julian Wyth/Alamy; 86(iv) Andrea Matone/Alamy; 86(v) Jon Arnold Images Ltd/Alamy; 88t Petr Svarc/Alamy; 88b Lonely Planet Images/Alamy; 89t Martyn Vickery/Alamy; 89c John Kellerman/Alamy; 92t Peter Barritt/Alamy; 92ct AGF Srl/Alamy Stock Photo; 92cb Paul Carstairs/Alamy; 92b Ian Fraser/Alamy; 93 BANANA PANCAKE/Alamy; 94t Lonely Planet Images/Alamy; 94b petforsberg/Alamy; 95t Paul Carstairs/Alamy; 95c Jorge Fernandez/Alamy; 95b CuboImages srl/Alamy; 98(i) Craig Buchanan/Alamy; 98(ii) Adam Eastland Italy/Alamy; 99 Matteo Colombo/Alamy; 100t Radius Images/Alamy; 100b LOOK Die Bildagentur der Fotografen GmbH/Alamy; 101t CuboImages srl/Alamy; 101c Sarah Quill/Alamy; 104c Chuck Pefley/Alamy; 104b AA/D Miterdiri; 106t Geoff A Howard/Alamy; 106b Alessandro Villa/Alamy; 107t AA/S McBride; 107c oliver selwyn/Alamy; 107b LOOK Die Bildagentur der Fotografen GmbH/Alamy; 110(i) AA/C Sawyer; 110(ii) CuboImages srl/Alamy; 110(iv) imagebroker/Alamy; 110(vi) OpenPhoto/Alamy; 112t I CAPTURE PHOTOGRAPHY/Alamy; 112b LOOK Die Bildagentur der Fotografen GmbH/Alamy; 113t LOOK Die Bildagentur der Fotografen GmbH/Alamy; 116t giuseppe masci/Alamy; 116c Ivan Vdovin/Alamy; 117 Images Etc Ltd/Alamy; 118 imagebroker/Alamy; 120/121b Ian Dagnall/Alamy; 121ct ENP/Alamy; 123 CuboImages srl/Alamy; 132/133t Cris Haigh/Alamy; 132/133b JTB Photo Communications, Inc./Alamy; 133ct AA/R Newton; 133cb Paul Carstairs/Alamy; 138 Terry Smith Images/Alamy; 140 Matthew Kawalski/Alamy; 142t Kevin Galvin/Alamy; 142ct Bon Appetit/Alamy; 142cb Chuck Pefley/Alamy; 142b Matthias Scholz/Alamy; 145l MARKOS DOLOPIKOS/Alamy; 145r Antica Locanda Montin; 148 Bon Appetit/Alamy; 152 Kumar Sriskandan/Alamy; 154t David Keith Jones/Alamy; 154ct Matthias Scholz/Alamy; 154cb AA/D Miterdiri; 154b Hemis/Alamy; 156l ENP/Alamy; 156r Adam Eastland Italy/Alamy; 160 Jim Ritchie/Alamy.

Every effort has been made to trace the copyright holders, and we apologize in advance for any unintentional omissions or errors. We would be pleased to apply any corrections in a following edition of this publication.